It's Health & Safety Gone Mad!

Alan Pearce

GIBSON SQUARE

For Rebeckah, 'Stay safe.'

Also by Alan Pearce:

www.alanpearce.com
Whose Side Are They On?
Playing It Safe

This edition published for the first time in 2009 by

Gibson Square

UK Tel: +44 (0)20 7096 1100
   Fax: +44 (0)20 7993 2214
US Tel: +1 646 216 9813
   Fax: +1 646 216 9488
Eire Tel: +353 (0)1 657 1057

rights@gibsonsquare.com
www.gibsonsquare.com

ISBN 978-1906142452

Printed by Clays, Bungay.

'Rules are for the obedience of fools and the guidance of wise men.'

Douglas Bader

It's All For Your Own Good

We no longer face the perils of the Donkey Derby, the danger of Christmas tinsel or risk 'trip hazards' from our own doormats. The State has stepped in to keep us all safe from harm.

We no longer fear banging our heads on hanging baskets. We don't have to chance our luck dancing on hard-wood floors. We have a watchful government on the look-out for health and safety 'crimes'.

It's hard to image the risks that our predecessors faced. It's a miracle that we managed to survive this far. Britons, it seems, are all incapable of thinking for themselves.

How many realise the dangers of baggy swimming trunks or the risks we face queuing for concert tickets? Even swallowing great handfuls of yew tree leaves can prove hazardous. Where once common sense ruled today we have legislation.

'If legislation was a guarantee of greater public safety,' says Nick Clegg of the Liberal Democrats. 'This country would be the safest nation on earth.'

Lucky us.

Thanks to the Health and Safety Offences Act 2008, what was once seen as a mishap is today classified as a 'crime'. Let your post delivery operative scratch themselves on your rosebush and you may face a whopping fine or a term in jail.

'The new Act sends out an important message to those who flout the law,' says the head of the Health and Safety Executive, Judith Hackitt.

'It is right that there should be a real deterrent to those

businesses and individuals that do not take their health and safety responsibilities seriously,' she says.

We must be prepared to sacrifice our traditional way of life and our age-old pastimes. Wave goodbye to the summer fete, and the May Queen, and ice cream toppings that may leave you quadriplegic.

Say hello to the slip-free, risk assessed, cotton wool world of Britain in the 21st Century.

Alan Pearce
www.alanpearce.com

Toppings tumble in ice cream ban

A LUXURY ice cream chain is refusing to pour chocolate sauce and other toppings over its cones because of health and safety fears.

World-famous Italian ice cream chain Morellis Gelato claims its popular toppings pose a serious hazard to the public if they fall on the floor.

The chain, with parlours at Harrods and Selfridges, has banned staff adding little extras because customers might slip over. Instead, they are serving toppings in a separate tub.

John Midgley, of the Campaign Against Political Correctness, said: 'What's the world coming to when you're not allowed to put a bit of chocolate sauce on a cone? It's symptomatic of the compensation culture age in which we are living.'

Publisher Sarah Kenning, 29, said: 'I've been going there for 25 years and I've never heard anything so stupid.'

Elaine Wienand, 29, said: 'As any mum knows, kids spill things all the time. It's simple. You clean it up and no one dies.'

However, a Morellis spokesperson said the ban was 'common sense', adding: 'The sauce is quite liquidy and can tumble on the floor making it dangerous for customers.'

Daily Express 31/1/08

Publisher blows cold on dragon

A LEADING children's author has been told to drop a fire-breathing dragon from her new book – because the publishers fear they could be sued under health and safety regulations.

It is just one of the politically correct cuts Lindsey Gardiner says she has been told to make in case youngsters act out the stories.

As well as the scene showing her dragon toasting marshmallows with his breath, illustrations of an electric cooker with one element glowing red and of a boy on a ladder have had to go.

Ms Gardiner, 36, who has written and illustrated 15 internationally successful children's books, featuring her popular characters Lola, Poppy and Max, says such editing decisions are now common.

'I was told, "You can't have the dragon breathing fire because it goes against health and safety",' she said. 'It doesn't really make any sense.'

Pointing out that classic fairy tales such as *Hansel And Gretel* or *Little Red Riding Hood* would not get published today, Ms Gardiner said: 'It's a sad reflection of modern society. I've had books published in Japan, France, Spain and Holland and they don't ask for the same changes. It seems to be in Britain and the US that there are problems.'

Who Wants A Dragon? is published by Orchard Books.

A spokesperson for the Publishers' Association said: 'We are aware of some concerns by authors and it is something we can talk about in the industry.'

dailymail.co.uk 18/11/07

Don't face the music

SCHOOL music teachers are being advised to wear earplugs or stand behind anti-noise screens in an attempt to protect their hearing.

The Health and Safety Executive also warns that beginners pose the greatest danger because they can play too loud.

Officials say the cornet is the worst offending instrument at 140 decibels – equal to a plane taking off. Other instruments that could do long-term damage to teachers include the saxophone, which poses a risk after just 15 minutes.

Conductors are also warned not to expose themselves to brass, woodwind or percussion orchestras for more than 19 minutes. Failing to don ear protection could breach noise regulations.

In addition to screens, teachers are advised not to stand directly in front of an instrument. Other suggestions include playing in larger rooms or installing special sound-absorbent materials.

The HSE also warns that the screen must not be placed in a position for the sound to reverberate back to the child, putting them in added danger.

Daily Telegraph 21/1/09

Sheep substitute for derby jockeys

CHILDREN have been replaced with inflatable sheep for a donkey derby for the first time in four decades because of 'crazy' health and safety laws.

The summer donkey derby has been a fixture in Llandudno for 39 years with children coming from across Britain to take part.

But organisers have been told health and safety rules mean they cannot put children on the back of donkeys for the 30-second race.

They were replaced by inflatable sheep and one giant toy orangutan, although the donkeys seemed not to notice the difference.

Races still managed to take place on Bodafon Fields in Llandudno in events organised by Llandudno Rugby Club. Although children were prevented from racing the donkeys they were allowed to ride at walking pace and holding a parent's hand.

Llandudno Rugby Club chairman Robin Holden said: 'We asked insurers if they could give us cover for kids racing on donkeys, but they wouldn't touch it. The man who owns the donkeys approached his insurers and they said they could insure us if the donkeys were walking not racing.

'We took legal advice about whether parents could sign a waiver,' said Mr Holden but he was told parents could not sign away their children's rights. 'If they were injured, the child could wait and take action as soon as they were of legal age to do so.'

Organiser Brian Bertola, a Llandudno town councillor, said: 'It looks like compensation sickness has spread to North Wales.'

Daily Post Wales 27/7/07

Safety rules ground falcon

RED TAPE has put an end to a stunt which would have seen the one of the world's fastest creatures swooping to Earth near Lincoln.

Crowbar the peregrine falcon had been trained to plummet from an aircraft at 1,500ft and fly to the glove of falconer Neil Mumby.

But the 200mph spectacle, originally due to take place at the Lincolnshire Show, had to be scrapped when an animal enthusiast lodged a complaint with the Civil Aviation Authority.

It had been rescheduled to take place at the Wickenby Wings and Wheels event but this was also cancelled.

Shortly before the show, organisers were warned by the CAA that they must have full permission for dropping an 'object' from a plane.

'It's health and safety gone mad,' said pilot Malcolm

Howland. 'We were hoping we'd be okay this time as it's an open weekend here at Wickenby and not a formal event.'

Now there is no further opportunity to see Crowbar as she has gone into an aviary to moult.

Lincolnshire Echo 30/6/08

Ice swimmers grounded

A NEW Year's tradition that stretches back to 1960 has been scrapped on health and safety grounds. Each January swimmers have braved the icy waters of a reservoir to race for a wooden trophy and raise money for charity.

But organisers have called off the event in Todmorden, West Yorkshire, after failing to obtain insurance. They said firms were reluctant to cover one-off events for fear of heavy compensation claims.

'There is no way we can go ahead without cover because the swim is a very challenging one. It can be a bit rowdy,' said organiser Paul Taylor. 'There have never been any problems in the past and, all in all, it's a great day for everyone – there's usually about 50 people who enter the race – but we can't proceed without cover.'

Local charities will miss out as the event, which sees swimmers dressed as fairies and reindeer, raises money for them.

Participant David Sutcliffe said: 'People are very disappointed. We can't believe this will not go ahead. It's crazy when compensation culture kills off the traditions we love.'

Daily Mail 1/1/09

Diving into hot water

AT 64, Alan Treece believes he is old enough to look after himself. Which is why he was incensed when a swimming pool attendant warned him not to dive into the water to start his weekly swim. After all, he'd been doing it almost every Sunday morning for 20 years.

But under new health and safety regulations, Mr Treece was meant to lower himself gently into the water.

When the retired civil servant ignored the instruction and got on with his swim as usual, he found himself looking up at two police officers on the side of the pool.

The officers ordered him out of the water and told him to leave the leisure complex. He did so but returned that afternoon to complain. Officers then turned up at his home and arrested him.

But Mr Treece's determination to decide the dangers for himself cost him dearly when magistrates found him guilty of a public order offence. The judgment followed three hearings at two different courts in a case that rumbled on for seven months.

After the hearing, Mr Treece, who lives in Erith, South London, said: 'I am flabbergasted. I have got no faith in the legal system and no faith in the police. It's a farce.'

The court heard that Erith Sports Centre has a 'movable' floor and anyone diving risked spinal injuries.

Mr Treece was given a 12-month conditional discharge and ordered to pay costs of £455 within seven days.

This is London 23/1/07

Studs get the boot

CHILDREN on a football training course have been banned from wearing football boots – because they are deemed too dangerous.

Budding stars picked for the scheme, which is run by coaches from Championship side Charlton Athletic, have also had their trainers prohibited and are instead told to wear plimsolls during matches on grass pitches.

Bedonwell Primary School in South-East London, which hosts the course on behalf of the football club, sent a letter to parents stating: 'Your child should have their school PE kit with plimsolls. For health and safety reasons, children will not be allowed to wear trainers or football boots.'

Catherine Turner, 34, whose six-year-old daughter Bethan won a place on the scheme, said the school was 'wrapping children in cotton wool'.

'When I asked why, I was told the football boots could cause injury,' she said.

'It's just crazy – do you think Bobby Moore and the World Cup-winning team of 1966 had to put up with this?'

She added: 'I was shocked to find that they are using a leather football – maybe a sponge ball would have been more appropriate.'

Former England manager Sir Bobby Robson attacked the ban. 'The irony is that football boots are safer than plimsolls – they are designed to stop you slipping and sliding and turning on your ankle, which is a common injury.'

A spokesperson for Bedonwell Primary School said: 'Our main concern was that the studs could cause injury to the children.'

London Lite 27/10/07

Forms first for rescuers

COASTGUARDS have been ordered to fill in a health and safety questionnaire before they can respond to calls for help. All 400 of Britain's rescue units have been told that they must first complete a 'vehicle pre-journey risk assessment'.

Under the new rules, the teams have to take the time to answer four questions on the type of rescue and journey they are about to undertake.

After first filling out the date and time, the lead rescuer must outline the 'reason for journey' and detail any risks the team may encounter during the rescue, including both future current and weather conditions.

The form then demands an account of any 'actions

taken to mitigate risk' before the leader can fill in a 'yes' or 'no' as to whether the risk is 'acceptable'.

The forms have caused outrage among Britain's 3,200 coastguards who are furious after a string of health and safety rulings issued by the Maritime and Coastguard Agency.

'When we were first told about this, we simply couldn't believe it,' said one coastguard. 'They are asking us to waste time in the office filling out this stupid form.'

Earlier, a three-man coastguard crew from Devon were disciplined because they rescued a 13-year-old girl using a boat that had not been passed by health and safety officials. The girl had been only 150 yards out at sea.

Mail Online 20/1/09

Cloud over sports day

A SCHOOL cancelled its sports day for fear of children getting sunburned – even though it was a cloudy day and a chilly 15C. Some parents had turned up wearing light coats and even carrying umbrellas in case of showers.

But a notice was posted on the school door cancelling the fun just hours before the egg and spoon and sack races were due to start.

'I called the school to confirm arrangements for sports day and was told it had been cancelled because UV levels were too high,' said one parent. 'But there was a very overcast sky, threatening rain clouds and the thermometer read a mere 15C (59F). I thought the world had gone nuts.'

Paul Stephens, head of Broughton Junior School, Buckinghamshire, said the Met Office put the UV index – which measures the strength of the sun – at five. That meant pupils would have been at moderate risk of sunburn.

'Our priority will always be to put our children's health and safety before looking a little silly,' he said. 'Our sports day was postponed in line with school policy, introduced after a sports event in which some children were sunburned.'

Ed Yong of Cancer Research UK said: 'Even though people can still burn when the weather is cloudy, it's a shame to cancel a sports day. Instead, schools should ensure there is access to shady areas and children should wear t-shirts and use factor 15 sunscreen.'

Sunday Mirror 29/6/08

School grounds angels

TEACHERS have banned primary school kids from wearing angel wings in their nativity play because of health and safety worries. They fear pupils carrying candles in the play could set the festive costumes on fire.

Headmistress Linda Mitchell said the school made the decision after a risk assessment. 'It is to do with health and safety – you have to be so careful nowadays. If the children are carrying candles there's a danger if they turn suddenly.'

Mrs Mitchell of Sacred Heart RC Primary in Paignton, Devon, added that in last year's nativity play pupils suffered scratches from the wings. 'We had wings made from cardboard and flammable material – some children got scratched. The other teachers agreed it was sensible not to have wings.'

But mum Mandy Mason fears daughter Holli, five – who plays an angel – will be upset at being banned from wearing her wings. 'I think it's awful. How can they expect the children to look the part without the wings? It all seems rather over-the-top to me.'

But Mrs Mitchell said: 'I think most parents would rather their children didn't go up in smoke. There have been no complaints and the children will still look beautiful. Anyway, theologically, angels haven't always had wings.'

The Sun 30/11/07

No song tonight, pianoman

A WEALTHY passenger was banned from playing a cruise ship's grand piano on health and safety grounds – in case he hurt his fingers.

Businessman Andrew Studley, 40, wanted to tinkle the ivories to entertain friends at the end of a night out on a luxury cruise liner. But he was stunned when a cruise official told him they did not have health and safety insurance for him to play the piano in the ship's plush bar.

Now he is taking out his own £2m insurance cover for playing the piano in luxury hotels and cruise liners. Mr Studley, a company director, said: 'I couldn't believe it when the managers told me that, for health and safety reasons, I couldn't play. They were worried about an insurance claim if I hurt my fingers or had some other sort of accident.'

He was a passenger on the luxurious boutique cruise ship *Silver Whisper*, sailing from Southampton around the Med with wife Carol.

It was not the first time classically-trained pianist Mr Studley has been banned from entertaining friends. He was playing for guests at the five-star De Vere Grand hotel in Southampton just days before setting sail when the management told him to stop.

Mr Studley from Cowbridge said: 'I am a trained musician and it is lovely to be able to put on a free show at hotels and restaurants with an off-the-cuff performance.

'But twice now I have been told I am not able to because of health and safety reasons.'

His playing has been compared to the light music style of Richard Clayderman.

'It's not as if I play like Jerry Lee Lewis or Little Richard,' he said.

Western Mail 4/6/07

Council reverse on bus bench

ALL Helen Greenough and Vera Clews wanted was a little bench so they could rest their legs while they waited for the bus. But when it eventually arrived – after two years of asking – it was far from just the ticket.

The local council installed it with its back to the road, and facing a decidedly boring hedge.

Elderly passengers say they get stiff necks from having to look over their shoulders all the time. And when they do spot the bus, they often can't get round the bench quickly enough in order to catch it.

A spokesperson for Stoke-on-Trent City Council said: 'The bench was put in this position because it would be dangerous to have it facing the road. Some elderly people are unsteady on their feet and would risk falling into the road or getting splashed if it was facing the road.'

But Mrs Greenough and Mrs Clews said the position of the bench on the busy Leek Road was 'ridiculous'. Mrs Greenough, 84, said it had become a laughing stock.

'We are nearly all pensioners on this road and the bus only comes every 85 minutes so you can be waiting a long time,' she said. 'If they can't do it right then they might as well take it away.'

Ward councillor Marjorie Bate said: 'I've never seen anything so stupid. I've spoken to a council officer who confirmed that it was put in that way for safety reasons.'

Age Concern said the decision to site the bench facing away from the road was 'extremely patronising' to older people.

The council, stung by criticism, has now installed what it terms a sleek, azure blue bus shelter. 'The new shelter is of a stylish modern design with two parallel bars so weary travellers can take the weight off their feet before they hop on a bus,' said a spokesperson.

Daily Mail 20/8/07

Council reins in dog classes

DOG owners turning up to a long-running obedience class at Loanhead Town Hall were stunned to find they had been locked out – for health and safety reasons.

Midlothian Council says dogs are now banned from all its buildings as they are not 'compatible' with other users, such as lunch clubs.

'We hold the classes twice a week and we've never had any complaints,' pointed out trainer Helen Watson. 'The caretaker loved having us and was really sad when we had to leave.'

She said the classes were run to Kennel Club standards and covered basic training as well as advanced skills such as agility. The group is now struggling to find a permanent home.

'At the end of the day, we're helping people out and keeping people safe,' she said. 'It's important people know how to train their dogs.'

Dog owner Margaret Henderson, 32, from Livingston, said she had travelled to the classes regularly for two years. 'I'm really upset and disappointed by this decision,' she said.

'I think there's a vital need for this type of training. It's really poor that the council can't accommodate these classes, when there are clearly problems with people not controlling their dogs.'

Edinburgh Evening News 24/7/08

Turn round in undies drama

PARENTS staged an angry protest after their young daughters were forced to strip to their underwear in front of boys at school.

The girls, aged ten and 11, were left in tears after being ordered to change for PE in a mixed classroom under a school policy blamed on health and safety regulations.

The headmistress of Hillside School in Baddeley Green, Stoke-on-Trent, said the children had to get changed together as there were not enough teachers to supervise them separately. But furious mother Dawn Bedford said her ten-year-old daughter Sam was reduced to tears by the rules.

'The regulations are ridiculous,' she said. 'The girls have always changed separately. No one has ever been hurt.'

Sam, who had a perfect school record, was excluded for two days because she refused to get changed for after-school football practice with boys watching.

'Sam was embarrassed and distressed because the boys kept looking at her and making comments,' said her mother. 'She is now wearing her first bra and taking sex education lessons. Don't the teachers realise how difficult it is?'

Headmistress Suzanne Foster has now relented following a petition from 50 parents. She refused to comment on her safety concerns but said: 'The situation has now been resolved and the children are changing in separate areas.'

In a statement to parents, she said: 'The arrangements started this term purely for health and safety reasons. I cannot have unsupervised children at school.'

London Lite 30/9/06

Binmen weigh risks

MUM Sue Jackson was stunned when binmen refused to empty a wheelie bin put out by her 10-year-old daughter – because it was too heavy for their lorry.

The refuse collectors told Sue, 29, that their truck's hydraulic equipment couldn't lift it. But Sue says her daughter Lauren had easily wheeled the bin outside her Rochdale house.

'I just couldn't believe it when the bin men said it was too heavy for the refuse lorry,' she said.

'When I rang the council, the woman who I spoke to started laughing as well and said she'd never heard anything like it. It's not even as if my daughter is really strong. She's just an average sized 10-year-old.'

But Rochdale council says that the rules are there to

prevent damage to bins. A spokesperson said: 'If a bin is too heavy, the crew may be unable to empty it because the lip of the bin could break while being lifted on the lorry's lifting mechanism. This could cause a health and safety issue and damage the bin.'

Manchester Evening News 26/7/08

Let down for disabled driver

A DISABLED woman who sued Tesco because it ordered staff not to help her to pump her tyres has won £1,000 in compensation.

Jenni Crowly, 52, said she could not believe it when she went to the superstore's petrol station in Mold, North Wales, and staff refused to check her tyre pressure because they would not be covered by insurance.

Mrs Crowly, who suffers from arthritis and fibromyalgia, which causes muscle pain, sued Tesco under the Disability Discrimination Act.

Tesco defended the move by saying it was a health and safety issue because a fatality could result if staff allowed a motorist to leave the fore-court with tyres inflated to the wrong pressure.

But District Judge Viv Reeves ruled that Tesco's actions were discriminatory and ordered the supermarket to pay compensation.

Mrs Crowly from Deeside, said: 'First they said it was insurance, then they said it was health and safety, and then a memo was sent around all store garages telling staff not to put air in people's tyres. They say it is a health and safety issue yet are quite happy for members of the public to do it.'

The Times 24/4/08

Lights out for Xmas fundraiser

PENSIONER Dick Sheppard has pulled the plug on the spectacular Christmas lights display he has arranged at his home for the last 17 years – blaming 'nanny state' legislation.

Dick, 77, has delighted the neighbouring children every Christmas since 1980 with his amazing garden grotto, made up of ten thousand light bulbs and 90 animated dolls and animals.

But after learning that to carry on the charity fundraising venture he would have to get a charity licence and spend a fortune on having the electrics tested to comply with new health and safety laws, he has put an end to the tradition.

'It's broken my heart but I can't see how I can continue with all the restrictive laws there are these days,' said Dick of Gloucester.

'This government is controlling everything we do, everything we say, every movement we make,' said the former garage owner. 'They are taxing us and grinding us down in every way and this is just another example of how they are taking all the fun out of living.'

Dick, whose displays have made £40,000 for local charities over the last seventeen years, also blamed the police for lack of interest in protecting his display and the donations it raises.

'I had the donations stolen twice in the early years when the money was put in a bucket in the garden,' he said. 'Since then I have invented the wishing well with steel bands and chains around it to protect it and a surveillance camera pointing at it.'

He says the police told him they were not interested in tracking down stolen donations. 'They said you shouldn't put Christmas lights up in your garden because it invites vandalism. I really am in despair – what has this country come to?'

This is London 30/10/07

Phone throne thrown

VILLAGERS who can only get a mobile phone signal by standing on a wooden bench could have their plans for a replacement stone platform scuppered – over health and safety fears.

Residents of East Prawle in Devon have such a weak mobile phone signal they are only able to use handsets in one spot – a local park bench.

In a bid to stop people crowding the hotspot, parish councillors want to install a £100 podium, which has been dubbed the 'phone throne'. The 2ft plinth would be covered in earth and surrounded by rocks to blend into the background of the rural setting.

But South Hams District Council has now warned that if the plinth is big enough it will need planning permission and be subject to a 'risk assessment'. Planners say the plinth may also have to include a raft of health and safety measures.

Council spokesperson Pete Osborne said: 'If the parish council erects a structure which is designed for the public for a specific purpose then they need to carry out a risk assessment which looks at what it is going to be used for and the risks associated with it.'

Meanwhile, residents have branded the warning 'barmy'.

One said: 'It's typical – someone has a simple idea and the killjoys step in. We used to stand on the bench safely enough. We'll probably have to wear safety helmets.'

The bench's unique ability was discovered by a holiday-maker and news quickly spread around the village, which has a population of just 200. The phone signal can be found only by standing on the bench and facing west.

The council became involved after an elderly resident complained the seat was too dirty to sit on.

Daily Mail 24/5/07

Paperwork smothers amber hunt

THE annual children's amber hunt at a seaside resort has

become the latest pastime to fall victim to the health and safety police.

The hunt has taken place for the last seven years on the beach in Southwold, Suffolk. But this year the event has had to be cancelled after the organisers were warned they would have to complete a risk assessment due to the danger of a child being swept out to sea.

The event involves up to 400 children paying £1 each to search the beach for 12 pieces of amber placed on top of the pebbles.

Children finding the fossilised resin are allowed to keep it and are given a camera to take pictures for a photography competition with local shopping vouchers as prizes.

The organisers, Robin and Astrid Fournel, who run the town's Amber Shop, have now also been told they need extra marshals to make sure children do not fall in the water or get hurt.

It was also suggested that adults monitoring the event should undergo Criminal Records Bureau checks to ensure they were not sex offenders.

'We just thought it would be too much hassle trying to comply with everything,' said Mr Fournel. 'It's a shame because it was a fun event for children and got them away from their computers and TVs and out enjoying the fresh air with family and friends.'

Mr Fournel said he had been forced to take out public liability insurance cover of £5 million in the past. 'Previously we only had to deal with one man from the council, but this year we would have had to go before a committee to authorise the event,' he said.

Daily Telegraph 27/6/08

Critics halt cliff hero

AN AWARD-winning life-saver has been banned from halting suicides off the cliffs at Beachy Head because he has not followed the correct health and safety procedures.

Widower Keith Lane, 57, has stopped 29 men and women from committing suicide at the notorious cliffs and his rescues have won him prestigious bravery awards.

But he said he is constantly under fire for breaking health and safety rules such as not using a safety harness. The window cleaner has accused the Coastguard and the church-based Beachy Head Chaplaincy Team of 'jealousy'.

'I feel very disappointed,' said Keith. 'I set this up purely for humanitarian reasons and to save lives, not to get involved in politics. I've had people swearing at me. It's very hurtful and upsetting.'

His life-saving activities began after his wife Maggie fell from the cliffs in March 2004.

In one rescue, Keith slid 15ft down a wet cliff face to save a young mother but claims he was criticised afterwards. 'I was lectured for not following the correct procedures and told I should alert coastguards before attempting rescues. But it would have taken them 20 minutes to arrive and she might have slipped to her death in that time.'

Keith stopped a woman throwing herself off of Beachy Head just seven days after his own wife's suicide.

He has now closed the Maggie Lane Charity he founded to raise money for research into depression.

Coastguard official Nick Jury said: 'Although HM Coastguard recognises Mr Lane's well-meant efforts, we continue to advise against untrained and unequipped attempts at rescue. All too often these attempts end in the would-be rescuers having to be rescued themselves.'

But Keith insists it does not matter who saves a life as long as it is saved. 'I've been criticised for the way I save people but try telling that to those I've talked into staying alive.'

Eastbourne Today 3/10/07

Flowers in red tape

A VILLAGE has been locked in a bureaucratic nightmare – over two small flowerbeds.

To the residents of Everton in Nottinghamshire, the blooms added a splash of colour to an already picturesque corner of rural England.

But to county council officials they represented a health and safety risk which had to be licensed and regulated.

The confrontation began when the village's parish council decided to plant flowerbeds by a main road. It was swiftly informed that a 'licence to cultivate' was required.

Villagers were then told to submit a health and safety questionnaire and a risk assessment for carrying out the work. Once these had been granted, the plans had to be approved by Nottinghamshire county council's landscape team.

The accident investigation department also had to be consulted in case the flower beds caused a motoring hazard. And, of course, public liability insurance – with cover for at least £5 million – had to be taken out.

Parish councillor Richard Bacon, 63, said: 'It's ridiculous. The expense of doing all this is totally out of proportion with what we want to do. Their response seems totally over the top.'

However, a council spokesperson said: 'There are many health and safety concerns relating to works on the highway.'

Daily Mail 16/4/07

Wrong way runner warned

AN 80-year-old former Olympic hurdle runner has been told he will be banned from a department store if they catch him running up a down escalator a second time.

Peter Hildreth, who represented Britain at the Olympics in 1952, 1956 and 1960, said he used to train for his sport by running up the wrong way on escalators and decided to try out his old training regime as his 80th birthday approached.

'I started doing it last month because I was turning 80,' he said. 'As a young man I used to run up the escalator on the London Underground. I used to do it about once a week as part of my training.'

But he was finally caught by the head of the women's underwear department at Elphicks' store in Farnham. He was given a stern talking-to by store manager Graham Duerden who said the elderly man was violating health and safety rules and setting a bad example for young people.

The former athlete said he has had his fill of his old pastime. 'I am not going to do it anymore,' he said. 'My wife will be annoyed.'

UPI 28/7/08

Prom goer cross at flag ban

A RETIRED teacher says she was banned from waving her Cross of St George flag during a Proms performance on health and safety grounds.

A steward told Rosalind Hilton to put the five foot flag away during the Last Night of the Hallé Proms event at Manchester's Bridgewater Hall.

She and sister Susan Stanyard were preparing to hoist the flag above their heads for Land of Hope and Glory in the rousing finale, having unfurled the flag over the balcony by her seat. But they were soon spotted by a steward who told them to put it away before somebody got hurt.

Mrs Hilton, 58, from Chester, said: 'When I asked the

manager why, he said it was policy in the Bridgewater Hall that you can't have anything hanging from the sides. I told them they were just being killjoys.'

Ridiculing the assumption that dangling flags were dangerous, she plumped the furled-up standard on the manager's head and asked him: 'Would that really hurt if it fell on your head?'

She said the interruption 'ruined the whole evening' and commented: 'Who wants to get up and sing, 'Britons never, never shall be slaves,' when the health and safety Nazis are making a mockery of our freedom?'

Daily Telegraph 30/7/08

On your bum

A FRAIL 82-year-old woman was forced to shuffle up a set of steps on her backside after paramedics refused to help because of health and safety regulations.

Ambulance bosses ordered an investigation after Ellen Summers claimed she was forced to pull herself backwards up steps and along a corridor to get into her house.

The angry pensioner from Bradford, West Yorks, said the crew made no attempt to help her get into her home after they dropped her off from Bradford Royal Infirmary where she had been treated for a leg injury after a fall.

It was only when Mrs Summers reached her sofa that they helped her into a sitting position, saying health and safety guidelines prevented them from lifting people – despite the fact Mrs Summers is 5ft and weighs just nine stone.

Mrs Summers' daughter Patricia Wells is demanding to know why her mother was 'treated in such an inhumane and degrading way'. She said: 'The trauma of the fall was bad enough but after having to drag herself into the house she was left exhausted and for a person with a heart condition this could have proved fatal.'

The paramedics used a trolley to get Mrs Summers out of the ambulance but when they reached the steps up to the front door they told her she would have to get off and go it alone.

Mrs Summers said: 'They said they could not put me in the chair because I could not bend my leg and it might hit them in the face, so they put me down on the second step and I inched up on my bottom while they stood watching.'

Mrs Summers is now so nervous of travelling by ambulance that when she has to attend hospital she calls a taxi with wheelchair access. 'I will only use an ambulance again if I am unconscious,' she said.

This is London 23/10/06

Safety rules save shoplifters

A BAFFLED shopper from Poole claims a security guard at a shopping centre told him to release a teenager he had caught shoplifting red-handed.

Locksmith Robert Franks was inside Wilkinson's in the Dolphin Shopping Centre when he spotted two youths placing items inside their jackets before leaving the store without paying.

The 28-year-old confronted one of the youngsters when the pair attempted to run, while his wife told a security guard what had happened. The security guard refused to leave his post and advised Mr Franks to let the teenager go.

'I am flabbergasted,' Mr Franks said. 'I don't think I'll bother in future. It beggars belief. I was hoping for help, but they weren't interested.'

Manager of the Dolphin Centre, Jerry Stampfer, said the security staff 'are not employed to prevent shoplifting,' but to 'protect public safety in public areas'.

'We cannot simply intercept a member of the public because someone thinks they have seen something wrong,' he said. 'There was an incident in the public toilets at the time and, if the guard left, it would have put the public's health and safety at risk.'

Dorset Echo 7/7/07

Whistle blow for churchgoers

CHURCHWARDENS have been told they must carry whistles to alert worshippers if fire breaks out during a service.

The new rules, introduced by the Department of Communities and Local Government – headed by devout

Roman Catholic Ruth Kelly – were revealed by two senior church leaders.

In a newsletter to local churches, the Venerable Christine Hardman, Archdeacon of Lewisham, and the Venerable Michael Ipgrave, Archdeacon of Southwark, wrote: 'Some churches have already held 'fire practice' during the last hymn, timed the evacuation and noted that in their risk assessment. Churchwardens should be provided with standard teachers' playground whistles for this purpose.'

And, if not a whistle, then they should have a gong or air horn on hand to signal an evacuation if a blaze starts.

MPs reacted with astonishment at the red tape being imposed on churches.

Conservative Sir Patrick Cormack, a warden at St Mary's in Enville, Staffordshire, said: 'This is more bureaucracy gone mad. Why can't people be treated like responsible adults and trusted to behave properly without the government sticking its nose in?'

The government has already been criticised after insisting that churches display 'No Smoking' signs following the nation-wide ban – a decision that left religious leaders bemused because, they say, no one smokes in places of worship.

dailymail.co.uk 29/5/07

Last post for Booze

ROYAL Mail has shocked customers living in a remote

community by announcing it will no longer deliver their post – for health and safety reasons.

Residents in the hamlet of Booze, in Arkengarthdale, North Yorkshire, accused Royal Mail of 'cutting services by stealth' after they were told the road leading up to their houses was too steep, and could lead to back injuries for its employees.

People in the hamlet's 11 houses received letters telling them deliveries would be suspended the following day, and that they could collect their post from the sorting office in Richmond – a round trip of one-and-a-half hours.

North Yorkshire county councillor John Blackie, who represents the Upper Dales, said: 'This is the thin end of the wedge. It represents a dangerous threat to services in remote communities everywhere, and it must be stopped.'

In his letter to customers, delivery office manager Colin Appleby, said: 'The road is extremely narrow, and if you have to reverse down, this is potentially an accident waiting to happen.'

However, the road to Booze is maintained by the Highways Agency and is not the responsibility of the people living there.

A Royal Mail spokesperson said the health and safety of its staff was of paramount importance. 'A health and safety assessment was undertaken and the report confirmed that access to a number of premises is a risk to our staff and, as a result, deliveries were suspended,' she said.

Planning consultant Daniel Child who lives in Booze said: 'If I can't rely on the postal service I don't see how I can continue to work from home. This is a real blow for the rural economy, which is already suffering.'

Northern Echo 1/8/08

Kirkie Steps get safety paint

FOR 150 years, tourists have flocked to Montrose to paint and photograph the famous Kirkie Steps – the picturesque sandstone flight of stairs that flank the historic churchyard in the heart of the market town.

But now the council has been branded 'cultural vandals' by irate residents after bringing in workmen to daub the leading edges of the steps a fluorescent yellow in the name of health and safety.

Sandy Munro, a spokesman for a local heritage society, said: 'The council have to be jumped on from a great height. I am all for protecting people and health and safety, but what they have done is over the top.'

Mr Munro said he had been left 'flabbergasted' when he discovered what workmen had done. 'People have been painting those steps or photographing them for years. They essentially symbolise Montrose. The fact they have painted these yellow lines on them is absolutely hideous.'

But a spokesperson for Angus Council said the steps had been painted 'as part of health and safety measures designed to assist the visually-impaired'.

She said: 'Angus Council, like other local authorities, is making improvements and adaptations to council buildings to provide equality of access for those with disabilities under disability discrimination legislation.'

The Scotsman 10/5/08

Toddler fear for sandal wearers

NURSERIES should ban staff from wearing open-toed shoes because they are a safety hazard, a former teachers' leader has said.

Sandals and flip-flops endanger both nurses and toddlers, according to Deborah Lawson, a former chairman of Voice, a union for teachers.

Mrs Lawson said that nursery staff are vulnerable to having bikes ridden over their toes or being tripped by small children standing on the backs of their shoes.

And the fingers of crawling and inquisitive toddlers are easily caught by passing sandals, she said.

'We are not saying nursery nurses should wear flat, fuddyduddy shoes that are anti-fashion. It is about wearing clothing and footwear that is appropriate to the job you are doing,' insisted Mrs Lawson.

Despite protests from the nurses themselves, Mrs Lawson insisted such a policy was plain common sense. 'Children get so excited and so involved in play that things fall over,' she said.

'They might have built something quite high and want to show you but it is just as much fun to knock it down, causing a few dozen wooden bricks to come crashing down.'

Daily Telegraph 1/8/08

Kids ejected in bus belt rule

CHILDREN attending a primary school in the Western Isles cannot get seats on a bus because of new safety rules.

Parents of pupils at Laxdale, near Stornoway, said youngsters are now having to walk along roads with no pavements.

It follows legislation requiring each pupil to wear a seatbelt on buses, ending a practice of three sharing a double seat when seats were scarce.

Parents accused Comahairle nan Eilean Siar (Western Isles Council) of ignoring their pleas for extra buses to be laid on.

Laura Morrison said she and husband Neil were worried about their seven-year-old son and 11-year-old daughter.

'They could end up having to jump in a ditch to let big vehicles past as there are stretches on their route home which are single-track and busy with lorries and buses but which have no pavements,' she said.

A council spokesperson said: 'The council has a legal duty to ensure children are wearing seatbelts. However, we are aware of the concerns of parents and are looking at alternative options which would satisfy those concerns.'

BBC News 28/10/06

Back break bin banned

HOUSEHOLDERS have been told to stop putting their rubbish in wheelie bins – because dustmen might injure their backs lifting out the sacks. Instead, residents must place their bags directly on the street for collection by hand.

The health and safety ruling by Portsmouth City Council has caused fury because household waste is collected only once a fortnight. Residents claim sacks left in the street can be ripped open by scavenging animals, turning their neighbourhood into a rubbish dump.

Portsmouth is one of the few local authorities not to have lifting gear on all its dustcarts, allowing the wheelie bin to be attached to the back of the vehicle and emptied automatically.

Residents have been sent letters warning them that dustmen will no longer take their rubbish away if they continue to put it out in the bins.

'It's unbelievable,' said William Smith, 38, of Southsea. 'I've used a wheelie bin for the past five years and now they say they're not going to empty it any more.'

Vince Venus, the council's waste collection manager, said: 'Crews in some places were trying to do the residents a favour by reaching into their wheeled bins. But we can't allow that to go on any more because of health and safety.'

dailymail.co.uk 17/8/07

Schools opt for 'home' trips

THOUSANDS of children are being forced to take 'trips' within their own school grounds because teachers are so scared of being sued, a government-backed study has revealed.

They are increasingly failing to get beyond the school gates on outdoor education jaunts amid fears of litigation should anything go wrong and spiralling red tape.

Instead, a class going to visit the school vegetable patch or looking for wildlife on the playing fields would be counted as an outdoor trip.

The findings threaten to derail the government's campaign to encourage more outdoor education trips, as teaching unions express concern about bureaucracy and potential legal action.

The National Foundation for Education Research study found that increasingly activities which are counted as school trips are actually taking place on school grounds.

There has been a decline in off-site day visits and residential experiences in the UK and abroad due to health and safety and risk assessment issues along with transport costs.

This means that visits to field studies, environmental, outdoor pursuit and adventure centres are now 'relatively rare' for secondary school pupils.

The Association of School and College Leaders says the government must do more to reduce bureaucracy associated with risk assessment and to protect schools from threats of litigation.

'The government and the new board must address the problem of court judgements that have given a new meaning to the word 'accident', placing on teachers often unreasonable expectations of foresight,' said John

Dunford, general secretary of the ASCL.

'Risk assessment represents a massive bureaucratic burden for even the smallest of visits outside the school. This paperwork must be reduced,' he said.

Evening Standard 28/11/06

Red tape wraps up tulip parade

AN HISTORIC flower parade that has been held for half a century has been axed thanks to one of England's more modern traditions – red tape.

Tulip Sunday has been staged through the streets of the world-famous bulb-growing town of Spalding, Lincs, every year since 1958. But now organisers say they can no longer afford the spiralling costs of maintenance, policing and health and safety demands.

The show will instead be replaced by a static display in a local shopping centre, a move that has prompted outrage from dismayed locals.

Residents branded the loss of the parade the latest example of bureaucracy killing some of England's most treasured traditions.

The parade of half a million tulips has attracted thousands of tourists to the town.

But a recent meeting of Spalding's Flower Parade and Carnival Trust, which funds the show via donations, declared the era at an end.

It said rising costs meant it could no longer find

sufficient sponsorship from businesses to finance such an extravagant, wide-ranging display.

This year's 50th-anniversary event cost £225,000 – an increase of around 25 percent on its predecessor.

'It seems we're dispensing with 50 years' worth of tradition because of nothing better than compensation culture,' said one angry resident. 'But what do they think can happen at Tulip Sunday – that a bunch of flowers will fall on someone's head? It's just absolutely ridiculous.'

Daily Telegraph 5/8/08

Cemetery chops plastic flowers

CEMETERY workers have removed artificial flowers from plots in Keynsham near Bristol saying they pose a risk to health and safety.

Graham Lees said he was bewildered when he discovered flowers left near the memorial plaques for his father and stepfather had been taken away.

The town council has now placed a sign at the garden of remembrance informing visitors of the rules, which also ban ornaments and plants.

Town clerk Elaine Giles said the council tried to take a relaxed approach to the rule but had to be more strict when the number of items left by families continued to grow.

She said items such as glass containers, candles and artificial flowers containing wire and plastic could be smashed or cut into pieces when maintenance staff cut and strim grass.

She said a tougher line was being taken in the garden of remembrance as there are no graves. 'In the rest of the cemetery, where there are graves, these items can be contained within the plot, although there are one or two graves where occasionally we have to write to people to ask them to reduce the number of mementoes.'

Mr Lees said it was only when he made inquiries with cemetery staff that he was told they had been taken to the chapel of rest because of a ban on artificial flowers, which it emerged had been in place for at least 12 years but not widely publicised.

Bath Chronicle 7/8/08

Belt up Santa

FATHER Christmas has been left more red-faced than usual – after picking up a £30 fine for not wearing a seatbelt.

Santa – alias veteran fundraiser Peter Finnegan in costume – was on his way to an event for Doncaster's Bluebell Wood children's hospice when he was stopped.

He explained he found the belt painful because of a disability but the officer was not impressed. Mr Finnegan, 61, of Bolton-upon-Dearne, South Yorkshire, said: 'It's a bit mean around Christmas time.'

The former greengrocer has been registered disabled

since he was hit by a bus 17 years ago.

'I do believe you should wear seatbelts but on that morning the damp was irritating my shoulder and the belt was a bit tight so I took it off. I'd just gone around the corner when I was pulled up by a traffic officer. I told her about my disability and she could see I was in my Father Christmas costume but she was having none of it.'

Mike Trees, from South Yorkshire Police's road traffic department, defended the fine. 'We fully applaud this gentleman's fundraising efforts, we too support Bluebell Wood and are happy to help people raise money in all sorts of different ways,' he said.

'However, the letter of the law says that if he is driving he has to wear a seatbelt – even if he is dressed as Father Christmas. As far as I am aware, had he been in a sleigh pulled by reindeer he would have been exempt from the Road Traffic Act and wouldn't have needed a seatbelt, although he may have been subject to air traffic control regulations.'

BBC News 21/12/06

Handrail of God

FOR centuries the word of God had been preached unhindered from the pulpit in the Church of All Saints – then along came the health and safety jobsworths.

Now the church has been forced to draw up guidelines after being warned by council officials that the pulpit is 'dangerous' and that preachers might be injured while climbing its seven spiral stone steps.

The church in the Wyke Regis area of Weymouth, Dorset, dates from 1172 and has no record of injured clergy. But the health and safety officers have now suggested the addition of an unsightly handrail to the 16th Century pulpit.

The diocesan authorities, however, wouldn't hear of it. As an alternative, churchwarden Gary Hepburn drew up his own safety guidelines.

These pledge that no one under the influence of drink or drugs will be allowed to use the pulpit. And the steps shall not be approached in dim lighting, by anyone with poor vision or wearing bifocals, or by anyone feeling unwell.

Those entering or leaving the pulpit are advised to make maximum use of the structure itself and the stone column supporting it to steady themselves. All of which appeased inspectors from the environmental health department of Weymouth and Portland Borough Council.

This may not be surprising – as Mr Hepburn is by chance a health and safety consultant.

'The issues were raised when a visit was carried out by council officials on behalf of the Health and Safety Executive,' he said. 'They were looking at the building and its use in relation to the dangers that might be present in a workplace, which is not comparing like with like, in my humble opinion.'

The Rev Deborah Smith, Vicar of All Saints, said: 'I would like to take this opportunity to reassure my congregation that I have never taken the pulpit while under the influence of anything except the Holy Spirit.

'It does seem a little draconian to be so prescriptive about what is a common action, which must have been performed thousands of times in far more difficult circumstances than exist at All Saints, but who are we to reason why?'

This is London 10/8/08

Leaflets tackle chip fires

FOR decades fire crews have visited schools to deliver safety talks and give practical demonstrations of the best way to extinguish fires.

Chip pan fires are Britain's leading cause of injury from fire and can only be extinguished by a damp or wetted towel being placed over the top of the pan.

But Devon and Somerset Fire and Rescue Service has now withdrawn the dramatic chip ban demonstration for schoolchildren in case it encourages them to tackle one at home.

Instead, the pupils will be handed leaflets and given instructions telling them what they should do in the event of a hot oil blaze occurring at home.

However, firemen and parents have branded the ruling 'crazy' and say children need to be shown how to deal with an emergency.

'It is the first time in 15 years that we have not had the demonstration,' said Mark Richards from Torbay council.

Daily Telegraph 30/5/08

Playground hugs off

PARENTS are up in arms after being banned from a school playground for health and safety reasons.

Mothers and fathers have been able to enter the grounds and even classrooms for years to drop off their kids at the start of the day and pick them up after lessons.

But they have now been ordered to wait outside the gates of Chase Lane Primary School in Essex or face legal action for trespass.

Kelly Raison, who has a daughter at the school, said: 'We were told we were not allowed to take children in the playground because of health and safety.'

A newsletter sent to parents warns: 'If parents continue to enter the playground they will receive individual letters requesting them not to do so. If they fail to respond, names will be passed to the local authority for them to take legal proceedings.'

Deborah Carter, head teacher at Chase Lane Primary School, said too many parents were overcrowding the school: 'We have been experiencing problems with parents dropping off and collecting their children from school and have received complaints from the pupils that the parents are overcrowding the site.

'I asked the school council, which is made up of students, how we could improve this for them. They suggested a 'Hug and Bye to Parents' area, which we will be introducing shortly.'

Essex Gazette 8/3/07

Medics wouldn't run to save dying boy

THE father of an 11-year-old boy who died after collapsing during a walk on the beach said paramedics would not run to save his son's life.

Company director Jim Poynton, from Oxton, Wirral, said he believed a more urgent response might have saved his son, James, after he died of an undiagnosed heart condition.

He said paramedics walked to the point on Caldy beach where his son lay dying, after he had been told to spell the name of a nearby road so the ambulance could find them.

'They would not come because we were on the beach and until we knew how to spell the name of the road we were near,' said Mr Poynton. 'Then the paramedic would not run. She said it was health and safety. We were shouting "just get here now".'

An inquest at Wallasey town hall, which recorded a verdict of death by natural causes, heard that James suffered from the rare heart condition arrhythmogenic right ventri-cular displasia.

Afterwards, James's father said he believed both the ambulance service and the NHS had let his son down. He said there were warning signs when his son collapsed several times prior to the day he died, but doctors initially said it was 'fainting fits'.

Liverpool Daily Post 2/11/07

Crews feel the strain

THE tradition of pallbearers carrying coffins at funeral services is facing a threat from Britain's soaring obesity problem and a raft of health and safety regulations.

With the combined weight of corpse and casket regularly exceeding 35 stone, funeral directors are having to use trolleys and lifting equipment instead of professional pallbearers and family mourners.

John Weir of the National Society of Allied and Independent Funeral Directors, said: 'Even five years ago this was not a problem. It was rare to have a coffin that couldn't be physically carried. Now it's every single week. Health and safety regulations prevent us from legally carrying coffins in many cases.'

Until recently, coffins were made 22 to 24 inches wide, now 26 inches is standard and many companies use oversize 40 inch wide coffins. With heavy oak coffins weighing around eight stone, funeral directors sometimes ask mourners to sign a disclaimer before bearing the weight.

Known disasters have included the funeral firm who couldn't get a casket out the door, the coffin that buckled under the weight during the service and the coffin that wouldn't close.

Some families are being forced to buy two plots and pick-up trucks are being used to transport large coffins.

One crematorium in Bath, Somerset, has spent thousands of pounds installing large cremators to cater for the increasing number of oversized coffins. Staff regularly turn grieving families away because relatives are too big to be cremated at the site.

Evening Standard 9/10/06

One stop shop stops scooters

DISABILITY scooter users banned from Corby Council's One Stop Shop on health and safety grounds are fighting to get the controversial policy overturned.

Members of the disabled community have decided to fight the ban, which saw 68-year-old pensioner Maggie Silcock asked to leave the shop in George Street.

Mrs Silcock, who suffers from emphysema and heart problems, said: 'We are human beings and I think this is against our human rights. If other shops follow the council's lead we will not be able to leave our homes at all.'

Health and safety reasons are behind the decision, with the council claiming the scooters may knock down other customers.

In a letter to Mrs Silcock, the council's chief executive Chris Mallender said: 'The decision to prohibit the use of mobility scooters in the One Stop Shop was not one that was taken lightly.

'It was agreed mobility scooters could be a potential health and safety risk in a confined area, especially where there may be small children and older customers,' he said. 'They could also pose an increased hazard in the event of a fire and endanger the scooter user themselves.'

Bill Hall, 71, who has been wheelchair-bound for the past 30 years, said: 'A scooter is a medical aid, and a need, not a choice. They preach inclusion, but practice exclusion. All we are asking is for Corby Council to help us to help ourselves.'

Northants Evening Telegraph 23/10/07

Alarm call off

A CALL to cut the use of maroons – rockets fired as a signal when lifeboats launch – has been labelled 'health and safety gone mad' by a crew manager in Essex.

Phil Oxley, operations manager of Walton lifeboat station, said stopping the age-old tradition is 'a tragedy'.

But the Royal National Lifeboat Institution (RNLI) said: 'This is not a ban, but rather a recommendation not to use maroons unless totally necessary.'

Mr Oxley said he was concerned at the advice to not fire the two maroon alarms when a lifeboat is launching to a boat in distress. 'It seems people think everything is dangerous,' he said.

The tradition of firing the audible alarms dates back more than 100 years. It is managed professionally by a crewman who releases the maroon from a special apparatus.

'The maroons are an important link in letting the town know that their lifeboat is out,' he said. 'We depend entirely on donations to operate the lifeboat station and anything which removes the links between the lifeboat and the town has to be a backwards step.'

A spokesperson for the RNLI said there were some health and safety risks regarding maroons. 'There's the potential for misfire and for debris to be blown onshore by the wind,' she said. 'Consequently, it's been decided to minimise any potential risk by reducing the use of maroons, and to fire them only when absolutely necessary.'

BBC News 28/9/05

Lift risks confine woman to chair for six years

A MULTIPLE sclerosis sufferer has been forced to sleep in a chair for six years because her local NHS trust banned nurses from lifting her into bed in case they were injured.

Mrs Wolstenholme, who is 5ft 3in and weighs less than nine stone, has been forced to sleep in a reclining chair all that time.

The 51-year old was diagnosed with multiple sclerosis in 1995 and had been provided with nurses to lift her.

But in June 2002, the Milton Keynes NHS Primary Care Trust withdrew the service because of health and safety legislation, saying three of its staff had been injured trying to lift the patient.

The trust said Mrs Wolstenholme's MS caused spasms which made her 'hazardous' to its staff.

Her lawyers say the NHS trust misinterpreted its health and safety obligations and focused exclusively on the risks to its staff. Now the High Court has decided she can be moved using a mechanical hoist.

Daily Mail 13/5/08

Plug pulled on community pool

KILLJOY housing officers are warning a father-of-three that a much loved paddling pool poses a health and safety threat to its dozens of happy users.

The 12ft inflatable pool in Croxley View, Watford, was erected by 39-year-old John Scott to bring the community together and keep children out of trouble.

Delighted to have something to do over the summer holidays, more than 20 youngsters enjoyed paddling and playing in the water for three days until an official from Watford Community Housing Trust asked Mr Scott to take the pool down.

The trust, which runs Watford's council houses, said it had received a complaint from a neighbour.

Mr Scott, however, claimed overwhelming community support. 'It's a disgrace. There have been no accidents, no arguments,' he said. 'What do they want the children to do, go out and cause mayhem and vandalism? There's nothing for children here.'

Local resident Louise Hill said: 'They are always telling us to pull together as a community and then when we do this they throw it back in our faces.'

Maggie, 24, who has been using the pool with her toddler said it was 'ridiculous' to take the children's fun away. 'I can't see what on earth the problem is. The children can't play in the park as it's filled with syringes so this is all they have.'

But the Trust's representative, Leigh Abbott, claims the pool is a health and safety hazard, causes excessive noise and was not allowed on communal property.

Watford Observer 1/8/08

Jail bird feeders warns council

YORKSHIRE Council threatened 12 elderly residents at a sheltered housing complex in Bridlington with eviction and prison if they continued to feed the birds outside their home.

Complaints that birds – including seagulls and ducks – were causing a 'health nuisance' led to a council inspection and then a sharp letter from housing management officer Deb Towse warning that the old folk were breaching the terms of their tenancy agreements.

'We can also seek a number of legal remedies to prevent you from behaving in such a manner to exclude you from the locality,' she wrote to explain. 'A breach of some of these can lead to a prison sentence. If you lose your home as a result of anti-social behaviour, we do not have to re-house you.'

Many of the OAPs were said to have been distressed by the council's harsh tone. 'One elderly lady was that upset when she read the letter that she couldn't stop crying, she was frightened she was going to lose her home,' said Ron Tyler, who spoke on behalf of residents.

'It was absolutely disgusting. These people are retired. They enjoy feeding the ducks and now that bit of enjoyment is being taken away.'

Some residents, including Violet Good who has lived at the centre for 20 years, refuse to be intimidated by threatening letters. 'If I have some bread in the house, then I'll continue to give it to them,' she said.

'I feed them in my garden, one slice of bread in the morning and one at tea time,' said another resident. 'There are a lot of people who can't get out and love to see the ducks in their garden.

'It is so upsetting to have them say we are committing anti-social behaviour.'

Daily Telegraph 29/9/08

T-shirt show feels safety clamp

COLD water has been poured on plans for a revival of wet T-shirt contests at an Oldham cocktail bar.

The saucy scheme to revive the naughty party days of the 1980s at Maloney's, in Yorkshire Street, has had a wet flannel thrown over it because of health and safety fears and the possible threat of legal action by staff and customers.

Owners Yesteryear Pub Company has been advised by its own health and safety managers that the contests must be banned unless all staff and customers sign disclaimers.

Disappointed managing director Tony Callaghan said the threat of legal action was proving to be a massive killjoy for bars. 'It appears that one key condition of staging a wet T-shirt contest is that people don't get wet, which pretty well kills off the whole plan – there'll be no more titillation in Oldham centre.'

He said there were numerous grounds for concern. 'We have been advised that people getting wet may sue if they catch pneumonia, that wet floors may cause staff or customers to slip and sustain injury, and some of the better endowed participants may cause blokes to drop their drinks.'

They were advised to drop the idea by their own health and safety manager Sue McCabe. Tony added: 'I have to accept Sue's point of view – she is there to protect the customers and staff from hazards and risk. But it seems that the so-called Naughties are going to be anything but naughty in our bars.'

Oldham Advertiser 24/10/07

Smoking risk to terminally ill

POLITICALLY correct NHS bosses in Birmingham are battling to ban a smoking room for terminally ill patients – forcing them to be turfed out into the cold to enjoy their final cigarettes.

The Sheldon Unit – a palliative care home for patients dying from lung cancer and other diseases in Northfield – is one of only two health centres in the region to escape rigid smoke free legislation on 'sympathetic grounds'.

But when board members of South Birmingham Primary Care Trust heard of plans to upgrade the smoking room with a new ventilation system, the whole scheme went up in smoke.

'It doesn't matter if patients might be terminally ill,' said Dr Chris Spencer-Jones of the trust, who also heads the British Medical Association's national committee for public health.

'That is not relevant because there are other units where such patients cannot smoke,' he added. 'The practise at the Sheldon Unit is unacceptable.'

The NHS has made a point of promoting the Sheldon Unit on its website as a service that provides 'choice, privacy, dignity and autonomy' enabling patients to die in comfort and dignity.

'It just shows how utterly callous the public health agenda in this country has become with some bureaucrat telling people at the end of their lives that they can't enjoy one of their only pleasures,' said Neil Rafferty, spokesman for smokers' rights group Forest.

'It is absolutely deplorable and disgusting. I hope they are utterly ashamed of themselves.'

Sunday Mercury 23/11/08

Station signals alarm over candle

THE railway station bar, once a classic venue for romantic encounters, has fallen victim to the health and safety police.

When Michael Leventhal, a London publisher, wanted to impress his date on her birthday, the longest champagne bar in Europe seemed to be the perfect setting.

So Leventhal, 35, made a booking at St Pancras station, whose 96-metre bar has been promoted as a perfect meeting point for lovers. He also e-mailed a request for help in arranging a birthday surprise.

Leventhal asked whether he could bring a candle and have it surreptitiously placed on a cake, brought to the bar and presented to his companion when she was least expecting it.

In its 140-year history, St Pancras has survived steam trains, bombing raids and a massive electrification programme – but a candle was too much. Leventhal was baffled to be told that a full risk assessment of the 4in children's candle would have to be made before it could be allowed on the premises.

Senior officials would have to give their approval and safety measures put in place, including a fire extinguisher on stand-by in case the candle burnt out of control.

An e-mail from Raymond Lay, the bar's events manager, explained: 'I have asked the station operations if we would be allowed to have a lit candle at the champagne bar for a birthday cake and they have said that we will have to submit a risk assessment form stating what the risk will be to the bar and the station, and what we will put in place to combat any possible risks.'

Leventhal was shocked by the response – not least because St Pancras was built at the height of the steam age when blazing furnaces filled the station every day.

'I was amazed that such a tiny candle could cause such a huge problem. It was bureaucratic insanity,' he said. 'I thought it was preposterous but very funny. It was a second date. I had wanted to treat her.'

The Times 13/4/08

Marching orders for organ monkey

AN organ grinder and his toy monkey have been banned from performing in the streets of a Derbyshire town after fears that they might pose a danger to the public.

Ripley Town Council has now banned organ grinder Paddy Cooke and his monkey Simon – who were due to perform in the town centre – after they failed a risk assessment.

The council has earlier shelved plans for a Punch and Judy show and a dance act. Mr Cooke wears Victorian costume as he walks around playing his organ, a copy of an instrument used more than 150 years ago.

'It's not as if I have a live monkey which might jump

at people,' he said. 'Mine is a battery-operated interactive toy. He's very realistic but no danger to anyone.'

Amber Valley Borough Council demanded to see a general risk assessment before letting street acts go ahead. It wanted to study a list of hazards and know how they could be made safe, and even how many people might watch the shows.

Labour group leader Geoff Carlile said: 'This is typical of bureaucracy gone mad. This was sprung on us at the last minute and left us in a difficult situation.'

The council was told the ruling also applies to dance groups, clowns and brass bands, including the Salvation Army.

The town council's summer entertainments programme has now been suspended until further notice.

Derby Evening Telegraph 5/8/08

Juggler in a spin over risks

A CHAINSAW juggler has been barred from performing in London's Trafalgar Square in case he hurts himself or spectators.

'Mad' Chad Taylor had been hoping to break his own world record of 79 rotations in a minute.

The American showman made his name in the US with his notorious Chainsaws of Death act, which involves him juggling three running chainsaws. But the Greater London Authority turned down his proposal because of health and safety concerns.

A GLA spokesperson said Mr Taylor's promoters had approached them with the idea at short notice.

'This meant that there was insufficient time to receive their final proposal and make a proper health and safety assessment in time for the planned activity,' she said.

BBC News 15/6/06

Pub gives pony trotting orders

A HAPPY little country pub in Marshfield, near Cardiff and Newport, was home to locals in need of liquid refreshment and a place to commiserate together. Now the new landlord has banned one of the pub regulars – a two-year-old pony named Morning Mist.

The mare was apparently a devotee of John Smiths beer and was a regular customer at the Port O'Call pub along with owner Tony Manton.

But new bar owners Graham Wheatley and Craig Thomas have denied entry based on the grounds of health and safety.

Owner Tony said: 'I only took the pony in for a laugh one day when I was trying to get her used to traffic and people but it proved to be popular with the locals. She liked to drink John Smiths. I occasionally give her a can of John Smiths now but I don't suppose it's the same for her.'

New owner and equine killjoy Wheatley countered: 'With the previous owner, when you opened the door to the pub you were confronted by a horse's backside. When you are trying to serve fresh, good food, it's the last thing you want to see. Ponies are for paddocks and fields, not for pubs.

'I have no problem with Manton bringing the pony down as long as he leaves it tied outside,' he added.

Bridlepath 16/10/06

Car park ban for learners

LEARNER drivers have been banned from practising their manoeuvres in car parks amid fears children may be run over.

Driving instructors have been warned they face fines of up to £65 if they are caught teaching students how to parallel park or three point turn in any of the 46 car parks in Gosport, Hants.

Instructors, who are also not permitted to use private parking spaces, fear learners will be more likely to fail their test as they cannot practise pulling into bays. They also argue it is just as dangerous – if not more so – to practise on the open road.

Steve Bonnick, an instructor from the Platinum School of Motoring, said: 'I think they are being really over the top and I can't understand it. I use the council car parks every day and we are not in anybody's way – we always pick a quiet corner.'

The ban was imposed by Gosport Borough Council

which insists the ban is in place to avoid the possibility of a child being knocked over despite the town having no record of any such incident.

'We launched a high-profile campaign to try and warn them not to use the car parks before kids broke up from school,' a spokesperson said.

'This is because of health and safety and the fact there could be lots of youngsters in the car parks over the summer.'

Daily Telegraph 5/8/08

Risk on the cards

FOR eight years they have met each week for a few games of whist and a bit of a gossip.

But now 14 pensioners have been banned from the room they use in a sheltered housing complex because of health and safety concerns.

The group, aged between 70 and 90, were told that the housing association did not have £2 million public liability insurance to cover players who were not residents.

And unless they were prepared to pay an annual premium of £250 – on top of the £1.50 they each pay for room hire every week – they were told they would have to stop.

Bill Corbett, 86, who plays regularly, said: 'Perhaps they think that pensioners will attack each other with the playing cards.'

The players used five tables in a small corner of the communal room at a housing scheme of 20 flats at Neville Court, in the village of Heacham, Norfolk.

There has not been an accident since the residents and their guests started their game. But the group was sent a letter by the housing association saying that the insurance was necessary.

'They don't understand why they can't have their friends over to play cards,' added Mr Corbett, a former sheet steel worker.

Freebridge Community Housing said it was common practice to demand that members of the public who take part in activities in hired rooms on its premises were insured.

Daily Mail 13/8/08

Cards clutter wards

NURSES have told elderly patients not to put up 'get well soon' cards on a ward at Frenchay Hospital in Bristol.

John Nickolls sent his aunt Edna a card to cheer her up after she fell at her home.

But when he visited her he was told she had sent the card home because she was forbidden from putting it up beside her bed.

Mr Nickolls said during a previous visit he had been told he could not take flowers on to the ward for health and safety reasons.

A spokesperson for the hospital said there was no blanket ban on cards or flowers, but flowers were discouraged because they could clutter lockers and hamper cleaning. He said nurses would ask for cards to be moved if they were taking up too much space.

Mr Nickolls, 73, said: 'We wanted to cheer her up and there aren't many things you can give to someone who is ill. I thought it was taking away something very important from someone who wasn't very well.'

Richard Cottle, spokesperson for North Bristol NHS Trust, which runs Frenchay and Southmead hospitals, said: 'Responsibility for cleanliness lies with the sister-in-charge on each ward, and if they feel cards on display by a patient's bedside are getting in the way of domestic staff, they will ask them to be taken down.'

Bristol Evening Post 4/8/08

Safe, not brave

HEALTH and safety officials say the wording in police bravery awards should be changed to avoid encouraging officers to risk their lives.

Helen Reynolds, a health and safety officer with Lancashire Constabulary, says the current phrase which praises officers for acting 'with no thought to his or her safety' should be toned down.

She suggested changing the words to 'fully recognising the risks to their own safety'.

'We need to recognise the bravery of these officers but we also need to emphasise the importance of keeping them safe,' she said. 'Safety does not prevent them from doing brave acts.'

However, Detective Constable Alex Challenor of Lancashire Constabulary, who was given a bravery award in 2001 after he was shot at while pursuing a gang of armed robbers, described the idea as 'absolute rubbish'.

Daily Telegraph 3/10/08

Beeb bulb blunder

HOW many BBC staff does it take to change a lightbulb? Just the one, it seems – but it must be a safety-accredited workman called out at £10 a visit.

The corporation's stringent health and safety regulations apparently ban the average employee from performing the simple task themselves.

The ludicrous process was brought to light by a staff member in the BBC's in-house magazine, *Ariel*. 'I called up to ask for a new lightbulb for my desk lamp and was told this would cost £10,' said Louise Wordsworth, a learning project manager.

'On telling them I'd buy and replace the bulb myself – bought for the bargain price of £1 for two bulbs – I was told that it was against health and safety regulations.'

The corporation has faced criticism for its complicated internal-market system, first introduced in the 1990s by then-director general John Birt. Under the system, internal jobs such as changing a lightbulb or fixing a computer are outsourced to separate departments which then issue invoices accordingly.

The result is a Kaftaesque bureaucracy in which the simple can become very complicated – and very expensive.

In 2005, it was revealed that the outsourced property management firm Land Securities Trillium charged the BBC an astonishing £2,500 to erect nine shelves. The same firm charged £1,000 to erect a sign and £5,500 to install an air conditioning unit worth just £2,000.

The corporation has come in for union criticism for making some 4,000 redundancies to cut costs.

dailymail.co.uk 25/3/07

No cake for Pudsey

A BRISTOL head teacher has banned hundreds of kids from baking cakes for Children in Need on health and safety grounds

Pupils were due to bake Pudsey Bear-themed cakes at home and sell them to their classmates to raise money for the charity but head teacher Tamryn Savage claimed the homemade buns would not meet strict hygiene standards and risked sparking allergic reactions among pupils.

The 1,500 pupils at Downend School in Mangotsfield have now been told not to bring in their own cakes for the national charity event.

'It's completely ridiculous that they have done this as baking cakes is perfectly safe,' said parent Andy Hawkins. 'They're killjoys who have spoiled so many children's fun and I just can't get my head round it.'

Sixth-form pupil Oscar Wafter, 17, added: 'We're taught to bake cakes in classes at school from the age of 13. It's so bizarre that they should teach us how to bake them and then suddenly ban us from doing it to raise money.'

The school said it feared ingredients like nuts and artificial additives, such as gluten, could make pupils ill. Instead, school cooks will bake hundreds of fairy cakes and gingerbread men in the canteen which will then be sold to pupils.

'I have a very important job to do and that's ensuring the health and safety of all my pupils,' explained head teacher Tamryn. 'I suddenly thought about this and realised that my kids have a range of allergies and asked myself what if one of them eats something they shouldn't?'

Bristol Evening Post 13/11/08

Teen ban in Hoover hazard

A BOY of 16 has been given the brush off by a cleaning firm because he hasn't had health and safety clearance to use a Hoover.

Student Karl Walker was also told he is not old enough to use hot water, washing up liquid and furniture polish or to empty bins.

Karl was hired by Apollo Cleaning and worked in offices in Chippenham, Wilts, for a week until a regional manager ordered him to stop.

He said Karl and a pal – who at 16 are old enough to join the Army and fire a gun – needed health and safety training to operate cleaning equipment.

'I just don't understand what's going on,' said Karl. 'How can I be too young to use a vacuum cleaner? It's so stupid. I want to earn a living.'

Paul Lundy, boss of London-based Apollo Cleaning, said his company was just following government guidelines by insisting on safety clearance.

'When an employee is only 16 we have to be very careful with the tasks we set them as their bodies are not yet fully formed,' he explained.

The Sun 23/10/08

Banner ban for veteran

FOR TWO decades Dunkirk veteran Peter Miller has proudly carried a Royal British Legion banner of remembrance at Westminster Abbey but in a cruel blow the 88-year-old great grandfather has been told he is now too old.

Mr Miller served in the Royal Army Medical Corps

during the Second World War. He was captured during the retreat to Dunkirk and held prisoner for almost four years.

'Really this is another example of health and safety madness,' he said. 'I may be getting on but I'm in reasonable health for my age and quite capable of holding up the flag without dropping it.'

An Army spokesperson said officials felt the veteran appeared a little frail. 'The regimental secretary of the RAMC has told Mr Miller he must stand down because of a problem with insurance.'

Tory MP Patrick Mercer, a former Army officer, said: 'It's a very good job that health and safety were not at Dunkirk when Mr Miller was facing the Nazis. I suspect the outcome of the Second World War would have been very different.'

Daily Mail 7/11/08

Risk in the woods

FOREST chiefs have overruled the Magna Carta to stop North Wales people picking firewood from woodland.

For more than 800 years people have been allowed onto common land and woods to gather firewood for winter. But citing health and safety issues Forestry Commission chiefs have ended the tradition.

The move spells bad news for people like Mike Kamp who has been collecting free fuel for his wood-burning stove for the last 12 years.

'The Magna Carta states that a common man is allowed to enter forests and take deadwood for firewood, repairing homesteads, fixing tools and equipment and making charcoal,' he says.

'But now they've stopped issuing licences and the reasons they have given are really flimsy. They are claiming there are health and safety issues and refer to a booklet issued in 2000. Nowhere in this booklet do they mention the collecting of firewood so why are they referring to this now?'

Forestry boss Peter Garson said: 'Forestry Commission Wales is keen to support the use of wood as a fuel, and the most appropriate way to do this for domestic heating is by encouraging the development of local firewood merchants.

'In the past we have tried to accommodate such requests and we understand his disappointment in this instance, but this is an area where we are subject to increasing constraints in terms of health and safety.'

Daily Post Wales 25/10/08

Health issues bar thieving magpie

A PUB landlord has had to bar an unusual regular from his premises for stealing food and beer from customers.

The trouble-maker – a magpie nicknamed Thatcher – has been told he is no longer welcome at the King's Arms in Heath Common, Wakefield, for health and safety reasons.

Landlord Alan Tate said the bird's antics had been

amusing to start with but the novelty had worn off. 'He started walking on people's plates while they were eating and we had to refund a few meals,' he said.

The cheeky bird first started pecking on the windows of the pub and fast became a favourite with the customers.

'He got more and more used to people and started nicking beer out of pint glasses,' said Mr Tate. 'His favourite is the Classic Blonde which we have on – he went mad for that. He used to squawk at people who used to hide their pints from him.'

But Thatcher soon grew bolder and started pinching crisps and then tucking into customers' Sunday lunches. He was then barred from the bar but turned up in the pub garden, but the problems didn't stop there.

'It was getting too much – he was too mischievous and he used to attack children,' said Mr Tate. 'He used to land on them and peck at their heads, which was funny to watch so long as it wasn't your kid.'

BBC News 20/7/04

No flares for sea rescue

COASTGUARDS have been banned from using flares in rescue missions because they have been deemed a health and safety hazard.

The Maritime and Coastguard Agency (MCA) says the devices, which are used to illuminate large areas of land and sea during night-time searches, could cause 'considerable injury'.

Rescue teams have been told to use 'safer' alternatives such as torches and night-vision goggles during land-based cliff and beach rescues.

'This is the most stupid, ignorant thing I've heard of. Flares light up the entire sky and aid rescue missions – something that obviously can't be done with a hand-held torch,' pointed out one crewman.

'This is over-zealous bosses bowing to health and safety nonsense – but they don't realise it could put people at risk.'

Flares have been used in hundreds of rescue missions since the First World War along Britain's 10,200 miles of coastline. But an MCA review found no 'sound operational reason' for their continued use.

A spokesperson said he was unaware of any incidents in which coastguard personnel had been injured using flares, but added: 'They are capable of causing considerable injury, and for that reason alone using safer alternatives is beneficial,' he said.

Daily Mail 4/11/08

One in the eye for Facebook

SEPARATE attempts to organise flash mob events through Facebook have been called off by police after fears over public health and safety.

More than 500 people were set to take part in a feather-weight mass pillow fight contest in Leeds and over 1,200 were hoping to throw pies in people's faces in Brighton.

Police had earlier been alarmed by an internet-organised flash water fight involving over 350 people armed with water pistols and buckets that caused thousands of pounds of damage to a public garden in Millennium Square, Leeds.

Organisers in Brighton are now hoping the ten-minute 'splatterthon' will go ahead at a later date with full police cooperation. A pie fight spokesperson said: 'It's not as spontaneous as it was but it could still easily be a world record.'

The current record stands at 70 people.

'We are not about oppressing people, we are not about running a police state. We have no problem with people having fun,' said Inspector Dave Buggs of West Yorkshire Police.

'The last thing we want is for a thousand drink-filled youths fighting each other and getting the wrong idea,' he said.

Daily Mirror 19/5/08

Clear path for veg thieves

GARDENER Bill Malcolm has been ordered to remove barbed wire from around his allotment – in case thieves scratch themselves when they come to steal food and tools.

Mr Malcolm, 61, surrounded his plot with the wire to stop burglars raiding his tool shed and vandals destroying his vegetables. Intruders have struck three times in four months, stealing £300 of tools.

But Bromsgrove Council in Worcestershire declared the wire a health and safety hazard and said it would forcibly remove it if Mr Malcolm refused.

'It's ridiculous. All I wanted was to protect my property but the wire had to go in case a thief scratched himself,' said Mr Malcolm. 'I told the council that only someone climbing over on to my allotment could hurt themselves. They shouldn't be trespassing.'

However, a council spokesperson said: 'When barbed wire is identified on site, we are obliged to request its removal or remove it on health and safety grounds as this is a liability issue.'

Daily Express 10/10/08

The playground payouts

SCHOOLS paid out nearly £2 million in compensation for minor accidents in 2007/08, according to a local education authority survey.

Manchester City Council paid £5,000 to a pupil who slipped on leaves in the playground. In Rotherham, a pupil who broke an ankle when playing tag was awarded £21,168. Bradford City Council made the biggest single payout of £48,808 for a pupil who burned an arm on a radiator pipe.

Another authority paid a youngster £13,700 after slicing the top of their finger off when they clambered on to a security gate and started swinging on it.

The use of trampolines was blamed for nine accidents, including one in Wolverhampton where a student got a £2,500 payout after getting their arm trapped.

Falling goalposts were also responsible for two payouts. In Birmingham a student got £9,000 after the crossbar fell on his head during a match. And in Cornwall a student was awarded £5,000 for a broken nose when the goalpost fell on him.

Chris Woodhead, former chief inspector of schools, said: 'Sadly, we live in a world where too many people want to make money out of the slightest misfortune. Serious negligence is one thing, but accidents happen and always will.'

In total, 131 out of 150 local education authorities responded to the survey revealing they had paid out £1,765,790 in the 2007/08 financial year in respect of 399 claims.

Daily Mail 6/10/08

Speaking Welsh 'too risky'

IT HAS long served as a polite and apparently safe greeting between Welsh speakers.

But now health and safety concerns have stopped council telephone operators from greeting callers in Welsh.

Union officials want to spare employees from greeting callers with *bore da* (good morning) and *prynhawn da* (good afternoon). They say staff usually speak only in English and the extra greeting could damage their voice.

Under the Welsh Language Act, government bodies are obliged to offer services in the language, and most councils and large companies answer calls in English and Welsh.

But now Vale of Glamorgan council has barred the greeting. It says that its move complies with the Health and Safety Executive's advice that call centre workers limit the amount of time that they spend on the telephone.

Steffan Williams, a Welsh-speaking Plaid Cymru councillor, condemned the ban as an infringement of human rights. He said: 'I can't see how saying *bore da* will do people in a call centre any harm.'

A spokesperson for the council confirmed that staff have stopped answering in Welsh after their union had raised health and safety concerns.

The Times 8/5/07

Spitfire tribute shot down

PLANS for two Spitfires to fly a tandem tribute above an Armistice Day Parade have been shot down by aviation chiefs.

Organisers of Bedworth's famous parade had booked the two aircraft for a fly-past to mark the 65th anniversary of the Battle of Britain. But officials at the Civil Aviation Authority have banned the aerial salute for 'safety reasons'.

The move prompted a furious reaction from Gil Leach, chairman of the Bedworth parade committee. 'I will go down fighting – just like the Spitfire pilots did all those years ago.'

Mr Leach said he was baffled by the CAA's ruling, especially as Bedworth traditionally marks Remembrance Day with either a fly-past or an aerial poppy-drop.

'In the past, we've had Spitfires, a Messerschmitt, a Tornado and a Mustang, not to mention a Dakota for the poppy-drop,' he said. 'Apparently, the CAA are worried about single-engine aircraft flying over built-up areas. But we had no problems like this before in Bedworth.'

Coventry Telegraph 27/10/05

Beach ban for Bilbo

BILBO – Britain's only doggie lifeguard – has been given his marching orders after failing to meet safety standards.

The 14-stone Newfoundland has helped save three lives but the Royal National Lifeboat Institution sacked him, saying: 'He would fail the resuscitation test.'

Bilbo, aged six, is a familiar sight riding with his owner, head lifeguard Steve Jamieson, on a quad bike at Sennen, near Land's End in Cornwall.

Mr Jamieson, 54, said: 'It's a scandal, an absolute disgrace. Bilbo has had fantastic support. He's had 6,500 hits on his website, been on TV and I've written a book about him.'

Bilbo is trained to swim around struggling bathers and after they grab the float fixed to his harness he paddles to safety.

The RNLI, which took over running beach life-saving from the council, said: 'We can't employ a dog as a guard. They are banned from the beach.'

Daily Mirror 19/5/08

Ladder law grounds speed signs

ROADSIDE speed indicators worth more than £100,000 are lying unused in Lancashire because council workers have not been trained to climb ladders.

More than 30 speed indicator display (SpID) signs, which show drivers their speed, are being delayed because police say they cannot teach council staff how to climb ladders to put them up.

The police took responsibility for recharging batteries and moving the signs to different stretches of road when six were first bought by Lancashire County Council.

Now, the SpIDs have become so popular, with 20 installed across the county, that police say they can no longer be responsible for them and parish councils are set to take over.

A procedure review by the council found its staff need extra training to climb ladders to do the job, despite only being around three or four feet above the ground.

Councillor Tony Martin says the signs are now 'languishing in village halls' rather than helping to make roads safer.

PC Ian Ashton, of Lancashire's central road policing unit, said: 'We are now governed by working height regulations which mean that anyone who is using a ladder needs to undergo ladder training.'

A spokesperson for the Lancashire Road Safety Partnership welcomed the involvement of the parish councils in the erection of the signs, but added: 'If the site needs a risk assessment, health and safety guidelines must be followed.'

Lancashire Telegraph 6/8/07

Aladdin rubs council wrong way

THE amateur players in a village Christmas panto had no difficulty identifying the villains of the show – and they aren't even in the script.

For 17 years, the ladies and gentlemen and boys and girls of Peterculter, Aberdeenshire, have staged a show in the village hall – starring themselves.

Now killjoy council bosses have threatened them with a police raid on the first night of their Christmas run because their show contravenes health and safety laws.

City licensing officials at Aberdeen City Council spotted an advert in a local paper for *Aladdin* and ordered the city's lawyers to write to the organisers telling them to cancel.

Organiser Susan Chappell-Smith said: 'We can't understand why the council is being so heavy-handed. The last thing we want to do is break the law, but we had no idea we were doing anything wrong and it's too late to stop the show.'

A spokesperson for the council said it had a duty to report licensing breaches to the police. 'The legislation is in place to ensure the safety of people attending public buildings.'

Daily Mail 28/11/08

No lunch ride for OAPs

A CORNISH pub landlord who offers senior citizens a free lift to his restaurant has been ordered to stop on safety grounds.

The Bullers Arms pub meal deal for pensioners in Landrake includes a two-course lunch with free transport for less than £5 every Wednesday.

But Caradon District Council said by using his own car Ally Yeoman was effectively operating a taxi service, which needed a private hire licence.

Mr Yeoman believes the current law should be changed. 'The authorities stay in the office and they need to get out into the real world to see what's going on so they can change things.'

Senior citizens said their meal deal at the pub is the highlight of their week and for some it is the only chance they have to leave their homes.

'If Mr Yeoman is generous enough to want to come and bring people in, what's wrong with that?' asked one pensioner. 'Somebody said the law is an ass and quite frankly that's perfectly right. It's such a shame and I feel it's very unkind.'

But in a statement, Caradon District Council said it had no objection to the principle of providing transport for customers. It said it had supported Mr Yeoman by giving him advice on how to go about the matter legally.

The statement added: 'Vehicles used for transport must undergo vigorous annual safety checks. Likewise the driver must go through a driving test and a criminal record check.'

However, the Landrake pensioners will continue to receive free transport, thanks to the Trathens coach company. Spokesman John Bettinson said: 'I think the law's ridiculous, so on behalf of my company I've offered a free service on Wednesdays to bring the senior citizens to their local pub.'

BBC News 28/2/07

Clam closed by council

THOUSANDS have passed safely across Dartmoor's Clam Bridge for more than a century – perhaps enjoying a frisson of excitement at the modest risk they were taking – but health and safety officials have now ruled it too dangerous.

To the anger of local people and walkers, the bridge at Lustleigh Cleave, near Bovey Tracey, is due to be fenced off.

'The Clam Bridge is history,' says Peter Liddall as he took one last, sad walk over the bridge. 'I've been walking here for 25 or 30 years. This is a little corner of heaven.'

The construction of the bridge is rudimentary – two large oak logs lain across the tin-brown water with a rough handrail on one side. It is narrow, a bit wobbly in the middle and when the river is in spate the water can lap over.

A new bridge has already been built downstream. Costing £35,000, its design could hardly be more different – all steel girders, machined wood and concrete pillars faced with stone imported from out of the area.

Retired GP Steve Price said: 'It's appalling. They should keep the thing open, maybe put up a sign if they want to cover their own backs, saying cross this bridge at your own risk.'

Devon county council said the Clam Bridge could remain in situ but would have to be fenced off.

The Guardian 10/5/08

Mourners to get rise

THEY are a long way from being Public Enemy Number One when it comes to health hazards. But that hasn't stopped health and safety inspectors doing their best to protect us from the dangers of benches. Thousands may have to be ripped out and replaced because they are just a few inches too low.

This apparently makes it difficult for the elderly and disabled to get up from them, according to disability laws.

Health and safety officials cited the Disability

Discrimination Act 2005 while inspecting a crematorium in Nottinghamshire.

Bramcote Crematorium was told its 40 memorial benches, which have seats 14 ¾ inches high, were three inches lower than the minimum height of 17 ¾ inches, and five inches lower than the optimum height. It was ordered to remove them all.

To make matters worse, it has also been told that when it replaces the benches, it will have to fork out £200,000 for new lighting so they are visible in the dark.

Jayne Allen, who paid £400 for one of the memorial benches and plaques to commemorate her husband Phillip, has now had both returned to her.

'It's all very undignified and quite insulting,' she said. 'I also think it shows little respect for the dead. I was furious when I first got the letter, but when I spoke to the officers at the crematorium, I realised that the problem didn't come from them; it's the government's health and safety laws.'

Crematorium manager Kevin Browne, said: 'We also have to pay to put the new benches on an elevated slab, clear enough space at the side to give wheelchair access and make sure all the benches across our 18-acre site are properly lit.'

Daily Mail 3/6/07

Cliff campers can't queue

FANS of Sir Cliff Richard have been banned from queuing overnight ahead of the release of tickets for his 50th

Anniversary tour – because of health and safety fears.

Normally dozens of fans pitch tents outside venues when one of his tours is announced but Sheffield Arena have banned sleeping bags and tents. Fans can now only queue for tickets on the day of sale.

Viv Johnson, 60, who camped out for two weeks to be the first in the queue last time Sir Cliff played at the arena, said she would fight the ban.

'I don't know any other venue who stops us from queuing for days to get the best tickets. We're adults. We've never had any trouble and after a cup of tea we're asleep by 11pm.'

But Simon Bailey, marketing manager at Sheffield Arena, said staff had a 'duty of care' which they would not be able to provide if customers were camping outside the arena for days at a time.

'We are unable to staff the queue to ensure customer safety and the area isn't suitable for people to be camping out exposed to the elements,' he said.

Daily Telegraph 26/11/08

Xmas lights too heavy

STREET traders in Clevedon have been told they can't put up Christmas lights because of new health and safety guidelines.

North Somerset Council said it was unsafe to attach lights to columns in Hill Road because they are not load-bearing.

Bob Hughes, from the local Traders' Association, said traders had raised £3,500 towards the lights. 'These rules and regulations are pretty draconian and probably unnecessary,' he said.

But a spokesperson for the council pointed out: 'There is a code of practice which has to be followed regarding installation of Christmas lights for health and safety reasons.

'The lighting columns… are made of concrete and for safety reasons it is not possible to attach lights to them, as they are not load-bearing.

'We do permit Christmas lights in other locations and work with organisations across the district to support festive activities.'

BBC News 16/10/07

Monkey tree chop needles residents

A MUCH loved monkey puzzle tree faces the axe just weeks after campaigners were told it was safe – because health and safety experts now say the needles are too sharp.

The 150-year-old monkey puzzle managed to survive planners and construction workers on the site of a new school on West Cross Lane, Swansea. But after studying two separate reports, Swansea Council ruled the tree a danger.

One expert said: 'It is my opinion that as every effort is made in this day and age to prevent children playing with discarded syringe needles, every effort must be made to prevent children coming into contact with these potentially, equally sharp needles.'

He also warned: 'The fruit could be a potential pedestrian or vehicular hazard when falling.'

As well as warning of the potential danger from the 'syringe-like' needles, a second report warned the tree could blow over in a strong wind. 'Should an injury occur, the authority could find themselves defending any litigation.'

Local resident Carol Crafer, who led the fight to save the tree, said: 'I am absolutely livid. The tree's needles are not that dangerous. Comparing them to syringes is ridiculous.'

Swansea Evening Post 16/5/08

Hospital cleans out old Teds

PARENTS visiting children in hospital are being advised to bring new soft toys in factory-sealed boxes to prevent the spread of superbugs.

The guidance stems from concern that toy fabric is a breeding ground for MRSA and Clostridium difficile.

However, it is bound to cause distress to children who find it difficult to be separated from their favourite toys.

Nurses are also being told to stop cuddly toys being used by more than one child. And donations of second-hand teddies to wards are being destroyed because of the risks they present.

Studies have found harmful bugs on toys in GP waiting

rooms, and research in 2000 identified the same strain of MRSA on children as their toys.

A spokesperson for Birmingham Children's Hospital said: 'Hospital-acquired infections are a serious issue and there's a tangible risk from teddies, even those barely used.'

The issue has prompted A&E nurse Hilary McGibney to develop a wipe-clean teddy. She said: 'A toy can give a child comfort during an illness so something that can be instantly cleaned and then given back to them is a real bonus.'

dailymail.co.uk 25/5/08

Bunting in red tape tangle

FOR MORE than a century, the inhabitants of Hatfield Broad Oak have marked their special occasions with strings of bunting. In recent decades, the colourful flags have become an integral part of the annual village festival. Now they will flutter no more.

The bunting has become tangled up with health and safety red tape, and has become too costly – and complicated – for festival organisers to erect.

The annual event in the Essex village, which includes a craft fair, a dance and a dog show, raises about £10,000 a year for local groups and charities.

Organisers seeking permission from Essex County Council's highways department now have to complete six A4 sheets of paper and fill a range of conditions, including attaching the strings to fixed points on buildings using stainless steel bolts that require rigorous testing.

Parish councillor Leigh Trevitt, 40, said: 'The conditions are impractical and impossible. Many of the houses are listed so we couldn't get planning permission to put stainless steel bolts on them. And we could not afford professional installation.'

Many people, he said, had suggested they by-pass the rules and let Highways take them to court. 'But a lot of the people who organise the festival are elderly and are scared of the bullies,' he added.

An Essex Highways spokesperson said: 'While we sympathise with the organisers of community events these guidelines have been set down after real events where people have been injured.'

'Our village is a little piece of old England,' added Mr Trevitt. 'And if we are not careful we will lose all our rights.'

Daily Telegraph 25/5/08

Workers slope off

TRAFFORD Borough Council refused to cut the grass on a slope where a young boy injured himself in case its own workmen sustained injury.

When Vanessa Crowhurst rang the local authority hotline after her son Jamie, 11, slipped and cut his leg on hidden glass in the verge, her request to have the grass cut was ignored.

'I rang again a week later and was told that a note had

been put on my complaint saying "No further action",' she explained. 'I was then told by the person who wrote the note that it was against health and safety to cut the grass because the incline on the grass was too steep and there was nothing the council could do.'

Jamie had been playing football outside the family home when the ball landed on the nearby embankment. His mother says the grass had always been cut regularly in the past. 'These health and safety laws are political correctness gone mad. If the law has been changed… then it needs to be changed back.'

A council spokesperson said: 'The grass on the embankment is not cut on a regular basis because of the dangers of working on a steep gradient.

'We are concerned to hear about this incident and are looking at whether the area can be planted out with low growing shrubs to further discourage children from playing in the area.'

Daily Mail 8/9/08

Commuters dig in over heels

OVER the years, everything from leaves on the line to the wrong type of snow has been blamed for causing havoc for train passengers. But now, rail chiefs are blaming high heels for accidents on station concourses and one of Scotland's biggest railway stations is asking women to think twice before wearing stilettos.

Network Rail's move has been branded an example of an over-zealous health and safety culture, but rail chiefs claim the campaign has reduced accidents.

The posters feature a picture of a woman's shoe alongside the slogan 'How are your heels?' It states that twice as many women than men have been involved in 'slips, trips and falls' at the station – and claims 'footwear problems' cause many of them.

'Every time someone has a fall we have to fill in a report,' said a spokesperson for Network Rail. 'With men, excessive use of alcohol is often involved. In other cases accidents are caused by people running for trains and not looking where they are going.'

Councillor Maxine Smith, who regularly dons five-inch heels, said: 'I would not see any good reason to suddenly swap my high heels before arriving at the station.

'This may well be a case of Network Rail looking for a 'get out' clause in the face of customers submitting less than altruistic insurance claims. If so, it is a sad reflection of the compensation culture in the society in which we live.'

First ScotRail had earlier banned running on platforms.

Peter Lawrence, chairman of the independent passengers' group, Railfuture, said at the time: 'Health and safety concerns can sometimes go a little too far and this is one of those occasions.'

The Scotsman 24/5/08

Brush off for Wicker Man

A BID to turn abandoned timber into a giant 'wicker man' style artwork and set it ablaze has been vetoed by council chiefs.

Artist Oliver Zurek wanted to construct a giant effigy from the wood, which was washed up at Cow Gap beach from the stricken vessel *Ice Prince*.

Timber along much of the south coast has already been collected and disposed of, but the wood at Cow Gap cannot be gathered safely so council bosses decided to set fire to it.

However, Oliver believes the abandoned wood should be turned into an artwork. 'I feel it's a wasted opportunity not to build something with it first, for example "the wicker man",' he said. 'I feel this could be a great community project for locals and could increase the artistic profile of Eastbourne, if promoted correctly.'

A council spokesperson said: 'Only small fires will be allowed in a very confined area to avoid causing damage to the vegetated shingle and wave-cut platform of the beach. We appreciate that this may have been an opportunity for local artists but there would be other issues to consider, including health and safety.'

Eastbourne Herald 22/5/08

Bin bend banned

STUNNED residents have been told to empty their

wheelie bins themselves – to reduce the risk of binmen getting injured.

A council has written to thousands of householders asking them to help 'take a lot of the strain out of the job' following a health and safety review.

Officials at Craven District Council – based in Skipton, North Yorkshire – fear refuse workers could injure themselves if they are forced to lift heavy containers called pods which fit inside the bins and carry material for recycling.

The two plastic pods – which have handles and look like oversized shopping baskets – are used for glass and tins.

Mark Wallace, campaign director of the Taxpayers' Alliance, said: 'This is a total dog's dinner. Do the council really expect pensioners to lug around bottles rather than the binmen doing it?'

Craven has a multi-bin scheme. One wheelie bin contains food waste, another garden waste and a third blue bin is for paper as well as the pods for glass and tins.

In a letter to householders, the council said: 'Unfortunately, the success of the scheme is having a negative effect on many of our staff due to the awkward height of the bins and the amount of lifting they have to do during their working day.'

One resident, Julie Ward, 40, of Cross Hills, near Keighley, said: 'When I think about it, I just crack up laughing. I think the binmen are being lazy.

'It's just so annoying that we've got to start doing half their job for them,' she fumed. 'They are worried that this work might hurt them, but I don't think they've thought about how it might hurt a quite old person to pull these pods out.'

Daily Mail 22/5/08

Trim your bush

A WOMAN has been ordered to trim back a lavender bush in her front garden by Royal Mail – because it breaches health and safety regulations for postmen.

Marie Zadeh was astonished when she was sent a letter warning her to cut back the garden shrubbery – or make other arrangements to get her post.

Bosses at Royal Mail said she had to prune the shrub because her postman was having difficulty getting to her letter box.

The mum-of-two, who works as a gardener, said: 'It's just ridiculous. I think these new health and safety laws are going a bit too far. It all seems so unnecessary.'

The letter read: 'We are currently experiencing great difficulty in delivering your post due to the overgrown bushes in your pathway leading to your front door. I have an obligation to all my staff to ensure their health and safety at all times and this is now in breach of this.'

Mrs Zadeh, from Hove, West Sussex, said: 'There is nothing in my garden that would cut the postmen and women or strangle them or do them any harm at all. If the postmen happened to touch a bit of lavender it really is not going to hurt him in anyway at all.'

Evening Standard 27/6/07

Own goal at safety day

A FARMER is recovering after falling down an open drain and injuring her ankle at a health and safety demonstration.

Tania Foster, 45, damaged her Achilles tendon when she stumbled down the hole at the event organised by the Health and Safety Executive. The mother-of-two, from Capenhurst, Cheshire, said: 'It would be funny if it wasn't so painful.'

More than 200 farmers were invited to the safety day at Grange Farm, in Churton, near Chester. Speaking ahead of the event, Tony Trenear, the HSE agricultural inspector, said: 'The day is designed to make farmers take health and safety matters more seriously.'

But Mrs Foster said: 'I think they should listen to their own advice. Now, because of the health and safety people, I am injured at one of our busiest times of year.'

A spokesperson for the Health and Safety Executive said a risk assessment of the hole had been carried out but it was not deemed a serious risk.

He added: 'The hole had been seen but it was up against a wall and therefore thought unlikely to be a risk. Unfortunately, we have been caught out by circumstance, but it emphasises the need to be vigilant at all times.'

Daily Telegraph 10/3/07

Flag snub to workers

COUNCIL chiefs in Bradford have been forced into a humiliating U-turn over the flying of the Union flag at half-mast on City Hall.

Supporters of the International Workers' Memorial Day were stunned when the authority said it was too much of a health and safety risk for an employee to lower the roof-top flag to mark those who died in industrial accidents.

The decision was disclosed in a letter to Bradford MPs Gerry Sutcliffe and Terry Rooney in which council officials stated that: 'It should be noted that the practice of flying flags from City Hall was revised two years ago to minimise the number of times flags have to be raised and lowered from the roof.

'One of the chief reasons for doing this was concerns for the health and safety of staff who have to carry out the operation, working at height and in sometimes difficult weather conditions.'

Jane Howie, of Bradford Area Safety Reps Association, said it was a nonsense to claim there was a health and safety issue about lowering the roof-top flag.

'Lowering the flag is either dangerous or not dangerous,' she said. 'And if it is dangerous they should not have to do it for anybody.'

Unison regional officer Steve Torrance said: 'It was diabolical that Bradford Council would not at first recognise workers who have been killed, injured or made ill by their work by simply affording them the same recognition they show to Councillors, Lord Mayors and other dignitaries on their death.'

Bradford Telegraph 28/4/08

Widower pulls wife's flowers

A WIDOWER who lovingly tended his wife's grave was shocked to be told that he had to remove all the flowers he had planted for her.

Leonard Walker was heartbroken to be told to remove all his spring blooms because of a council regulation.

Witney Town Council blamed health and safety rules and said having plain grass would enable easier maintenance of its Windrush Cemetery.

But Mr Walker, 66, who has now removed the plants, said the council had destroyed all the loving care he had put into looking after the site since his wife Margaret died.

'She died last year, and I have been coming here every day to remember her and tend the grave. This makes me really sad and angry,' he said. 'I'd put bulbs in and some angels with lights. But they told me it all had to come out, just to put it to grass.'

Janine Howells, the council's amenities manager, said: 'Mr Walker was told about the rules. We have been very compassionate with him.'

Oxford Mail 20/5/08

Police escort for tree lover

POLICE had to escort a school governor from the grounds of his school when he tried to halt workmen cutting down one of Lancing's tallest trees.

The tree has stood in front of Oakfield Middle School for more than half a century. Five trees were planted when the original school was built – now only one remains following the Great Storm of 1987.

Councillor Keith Dollemore has been helping residents in their fight to keep the Lombardi tree from being cut down.

West Sussex County Council fear the tree is unstable and an obstruction to building work on the site. A spokesperson said: 'We are concerned that this poplar tree has dead wood in its crown and represents a potential risk to children, property and residents.

'Further discussions are taking place about whether the tree should be removed due to health and safety concerns.'

Mr Dollemore said: 'The tree is of historic interest. It's known to generations of local residents and children who have been to the school. We can't see any good reason to cut it down.'

West Sussex Gazette 21/5/08

Egg hatch lesson crushed

A PRIMARY school abandoned plans to hatch chicks in a classroom incubator because of 'ludicrous' health and safety rules. Teacher Jean Williams wanted seven-year-olds to see how the birds developed from six eggs.

But council health and safety officers insisted biological,

electrical, child and teacher risk assessments would first have to be carried out.

Kevin Bullock, head of Fordham school, near Ely, Cambridgeshire, was also told he would have to guarantee the eggs were salmonella-free.

County council officers demanded to know if children would be touching the eggs, if the incubator had a current safety certificate, and what the 'protocol' was for school holidays and weekends.

The final question seemed to miss the whole point. It asked: 'Do you intend to keep the incubator in school until the eggs are hatched?'

Mr Bullock said: 'It's one example of the ludicrous health and safety issues schools have to deal with.'

Daily Mail 23/5/08

Bottle feeder blocks way

A MUM was moved on from Ashton Town Hall steps while bottle feeding her baby by an angry security guard citing health and safety risks.

Tina Philburn sat on the steps in desperation after failing to find a seat free of smokers to feed 11-week-old daughter, Skye. But she says she was told by a security guard to 'move or be moved'.

'We'd been wandering around for a while but there wasn't a single place, it was full of people smoking,' she said. 'I didn't want my baby breathing in cigarette smoke so I thought the side of the steps would be a convenient place but within seconds a security guard came over and asked me what I thought I was doing.'

She added: 'It's disgusting that I was spoken to like that. I could understand it if I was some yob and there were 20 of us but I was just trying to feed my baby.'

A spokesperson for Tameside Council said: 'It is important to keep the town hall steps clear at peak times as they are the building's main evacuation route,' he said.

'However, with regard to the allegation that our guard was rude to this person, we can only apologise. We encourage our staff to be polite and courteous at all times.'

But Tina insists: 'I'll come home from now on and feed Skye where I know I won't be shouted at.'

Tameside Advertiser 21/5/08

Binmen's cold shoulder

FIRST there was the farce of homeowners being fined for failing to recycle the correct rubbish. Then there were the people scolded for simply leaving their wheelie bin lids open. Now one town hall has found yet another way to infuriate taxpaying residents waiting for their waste to be collected.

City of York Council is refusing to take away refuse because it is too cold.

They say health and safety legislation forbids their bin men from scooping out garden waste from the bottom of green bins with their hands if the grass cuttings, leaves and compost inside are frozen.

Instead all refuse must be collected mechanically by the lorry.

Hayley Parson, 21, from Clifton, York, said: 'I think it's rubbish. There must be some way they'd be able to get it out of the bin. It's just ridiculous.'

Another resident, Bev Smethers, 25, added: 'It's coming into winter so the council have got to expect frost. It's another case of bureaucracy at it's finest.'

A spokesperson for the City of York council defended the bin men's actions. 'At this time of year, as gardeners tidy up their gardens, we find that a good deal of woody material is placed in the bin,' she said.

'Our crews use the mechanical shaker on the bins to try and free as much of the waste as possible, but they are not allowed to reach into the bin to free the waste. Every effort is made to empty bins whilst adhering to necessary health and safety rules.'

Mail on Sunday 23/11/06

Fund dog in loo ban

A DOG who helped raise money for a town clock appeal with her toilet attendant owner has been banned from his public convenience.

Jack Russell Trixie was contravening health and safety rules while at work with Chris Foster, said Powys Council, which runs the toilets in Machynlleth.

It flushed out Trixie when the story of her fund-raising efforts appeared in a newspaper. Now Mr Foster has been told to leave the two-year-old terrier at home.

He said Powys Council feared Trixie could bite someone, but he added his dog was more likely to lick them. Trixie has been going to work with Mr Foster for the past month and they have raised £72 towards Machynlleth's town clock restoration appeal.

Mr Foster, 24, said: 'During the summer we can get 500 visitors a day to the toilet block and in a month I've only had two people who said they didn't like dogs. It looks like I'll have to leave Trixie locked up at home from now on because my partner works too.'

A spokesperson for Powys Council said: 'The toilet attendant has been told by his supervisor that it is against council policy to bring pets into council buildings.'

BBC News 30/8/05

Blind eye to stowaways

BRITISH border guards in Calais have been banned from using X-rays to search for illegal immigrants in lorries – unless they ask for the stowaways' written permission. French authorities have blocked the use of the scanners, claiming they could breach European health and safety laws.

They have told British immigration officials that if they want to use the machines they will first have to clear it with those they are looking for.

Given that the illegal immigrants do not want to be found, the chances of reaching such an agreement are zero, leaving the British no choice but to stop using the machines.

Immigration officials are said to be baffled by the decision.

The scanners – which have helped cut the number of illegal immigrants arriving in Dover by 88 percent – emit less radiation than an ordinary hospital X-ray and are used elsewhere in Europe with great success.

Adam Holloway, Conservative MP for Gravesham, Kent, said: 'This appears extremely convenient for the French authorities who, once again, have come up with an excuse to move the problem of immigration control over to British soil. It's also yet another clear example of European Union overregulation.'

Daily Mail 23/1/08

Safety excuse bars snappers

TOWER Hamlets council in East London banned press photographers from two local council by-election counts citing health and safety reasons saying the room wasn't big enough.

The *East London Advertiser* said it was the fourth election running in which the authority had banned its photographers from taking pictures of the count at the Excel Centre in London's Docklands.

Deputy editor Ted Jeory said the count rooms were large enough and that the health and safety claim was a 'smokescreen' for council fears that photographers would take the 'wrong' kind of pictures. He accused council authorities of behaving like they were in an 'old Soviet Republic'.

Kelly Rickard, from the council's communications department, said the council was following standard practice and that it had given the *Advertiser* 'plenty of advance warning' of the ban.

According to the paper, the council previously banned all press photographers from the count at the Shadwell by-election in 2007, the borough-wide Town Hall elections in 2006 and the general election in 2005.

Press Gazette 2/5/08

Insurance slays Santa

TRADITION has it that Father Christmas travels by sleigh but it seems even he is not exempt from the diktats of the health and safety police. They have told one Santa that he must be strapped into a full body harness in case he falls out of his sleigh as it is towed by a Land Rover at the gentle speed of five miles an hour.

Members of the Halesowen and Rowley Regis Rotary Club were told that they would have to raise a four-figure sum to cover the insurance costs of a visit by Father Christmas, until he agreed to belt up.

Barry Wheeler, the president of the West Midlands club, said: 'Every year we have made sure Santa gets to go through the town and wave to the children. It just seemed ridiculous, especially because he doesn't actually ride on the sleigh that often. He would be more likely to injure himself getting in and out of the sleigh than actually falling out of it.'

One of the members of the club, which has been organising visits by Father Christmas for the past 20 years, has now taken the sleigh to be fitted with the harness. This means the club saved £200 on its insurance policy and could still go ahead with the event. However, members said the tough rules took 'the magic out of Christmas'.

'We're going to try to make the belt as discreet as possible,' said Mr Wheeler. 'The sleigh ride through the towns starts in December and starts Christmas off for so many people. It would have been such a shame to see it cancelled.'

Daily Telegraph 19/4/08

Council dampens BBQ ardour

HEALTH and safety chiefs are pouring cold water on Britain's barbecues in case people get killed or injured.

London's Camden council has ruled professional caterers must be hired to run coal barbecues at community events even though hard-up local groups cannot afford the expense.

Safety chiefs also say those operating gas cookers will have to complete a course to gain health and safety qualifications.

Labour councillor Pat Callaghan, who helps with the Primrose Hill festival in Chalcot Square every June, described the decision as an over-reaction.

'To back professional caterers over local people almost defeats the purpose of having a festival. The area is supervised and there have been no accidents. It's madness.'

Volunteer Keith Bird, who has run the Primrose Hill barbecue for 25 years, is furious at the loss of his chef role. 'It is so patronising to have to go on one of these courses. I am not an irresponsible or stupid person.'

The council say public safety is at risk from the stalls and that barbecue users damage grass by emptying coal on the ground.

Daily Mail 3/5/08

Bin block puts mum in dock

A MUM'S long-running wrangle with a council over a wheelie bin may now end up in court. Sharon Bawden and Middlesbrough Council have been locked in a stand-off for the past four years.

The mum-of-two, who is recovering from an operation to remove her gall bladder, said she has great difficulty pulling her bin up her steep drive.

'The drive is a one-in-five gradient,' she said. 'I have

always had difficulty pulling the wheelie bin up it when it is full. It's very heavy and I have slipped and hurt myself.'

To bring the dispute to a head, she has now had her own risk assessment carried out, saying: 'It breaches health and safety law. It is dangerous.'

She wants the council to provide an assisted refuse collection or allow her to continue using black sacks.

A council spokesperson said: 'Ms Bawden does have a long-standing complaint in respect of the repositioning of her wheeled bin after collection, which on occasion has blocked access to her driveway.'

He said the council had agreed to continue to collect black bags from the house until the result of a hearing by the Complaints and Appeals Committee.

But Mrs Bawden fears the worse. 'They are saying they are going to take me to court and I will end up with a criminal record.'

Evening Gazette 12/5/08

Parents fume at 10 pound fee to collect kids

PARENTS hoping to pick up their children from a Scout jamboree in Devon were surprised to be charged a £10 health and safety fee to cover the costs of safely supervising the half-mile drive at Woodlands Leisure Park

Several scout officials and dozens of parents found themselves locked in heated arguments with park staff who refused to back down.

'It was a dangerous situation. I've never known anything like it. It was chaos and very dangerous for all the children,' said Scout Leader Steve Drake.

Parents said hundreds of Scouts aged 11-17 were 'milling around' the car park and driveway and described the situation as 'very ugly'.

'We had trouble keeping track of where children were,' said Mr Drake. 'They told us it was for health and safety but it was even more dangerous than it should have been. We called for the assistant manager but he wouldn't budge.'

Woodlands spokesperson Sally Williams said charging for parking is in line with company health and safety policy.

'This is the park's normal policy. People can't go through with their cars without paying the entrance fee,' she explained. 'It is a health and safety issue and has been in place for years. It's definitely not a new thing.'

Daily Mail 26/9/08

Silent salute

ON the grounds of health and safety, the traditional firing of a Remembrance Sunday salute has been banned in the seaside town of Walton in Essex.

Maroons fired by lifeboatmen to mark the beginning and the end of the two-minute silence could, apparently, misfire. Worse, the debris could be blown back to shore by the wind, where there is an infinitesimal chance of it damaging property or onlookers.

Daily Mirror 9/11/05

Firefighters snub home smokers

THEY are trained to brave every kind of danger to safeguard the public but now firefighters are being ordered to turn back if they encounter a cloud of smoke – from a cigarette.

Fire crews have been banned from making home visits to offer safety advice to people who smoke, unless the residents stub out all cigarettes at least one hour beforehand and open their windows.

The official edict was sent out by fire brigade chiefs in order to comply with the workplace smoking ban – after they decided that private homes filled with cigarette smoke are officially a firefighter's workplace for the duration of the visit.

Officials stressed that the new rules would only apply to prearranged 'Home Fire Safety Visits', and not to emergencies in which homes were actually burning down. But firefighters say the memo typified a growing obsession with petty health and safety technicalities and political correctness.

The latest no-smoking rules were sent out by London Fire Brigade chiefs to all staff, setting out new conditions for carrying out home visits, during which firefighters advise on all aspects of safety as well as fitting or checking smoke alarms.

One firefighter who asked not to be named, said: 'This stuff is what senior officers now seem to think is important. Where's the common sense? If we turn up to a house and it's a bit smoky we can probably ask them to open a window. Do we really need a new set of official regulations to cover it?'

Daily Mail 21/2/08

Shot gull shocks shoppers

A SHOPPER has told of his shock after coming across a seagull dying of a gunshot wound in a busy town centre street.

James McFadden was walking along King Street in South Shields when he saw the bird bleeding heavily from its chest outside the NatWest Bank.

'The poor thing was delirious, and there was a hole in its chest which looked to have been caused by a gunshot,' the 39-year-old said. 'Not only was it upsetting for myself, and everyone else who witnessed the bird dying, but it's awful to think how long it had to suffer in agony.'

A council spokesperson confirmed a contractor had carried out a cull that morning. However, he added that the location and time at which the bird was found made it 'extremely unlikely' it was harmed as a result of the cull.

He said: 'Culls are only carried out in exceptional circumstances, where seagulls are causing significant problems in terms of nuisance or public health and safety.'

An eight-year-old girl from Simonside, South Shields, was also horrified by the incident. 'I felt sick,' she said. 'It was so sad the bird was hurting. I never want to see a bird in pain or agony again.'

After waiting for 45 minutes and watching the bird die, Mr McFadden returned to work, by which time passers-by had covered the seagull with a towel.

The Shields Gazette 25/4/08

Anger over cab correctness

AFTER years covering the streets on their patch, most taxi drivers think they know the business inside out. But now they have been told the knowledge is not enough – they must go back to school and learn how to lift cases, greet customers and assess their body language.

Cabbies in Bournemouth are furious after more than 100 of them were suspended for failing to take a health and safety exam. One driver, who has passed the test, said: 'It's an idiot's course. It's ridiculous.'

The course also covers licensing regulations plus route planning and disability awareness. Cabbies must attend eight two-hour classes and are given three text books to help them revise. One book has a diagram on how to talk to passengers.

Green speech bubbles give three examples of how to greet a passenger – 'Hello Mrs Smith', or 'Nice to see you again' and 'Good morning, how are you?'

But 101 cabbies who refused to sign up to the scheme have had their licences suspended. 'I've been driving a cab for 25 years so why should I have to prove I'm capable of the doing the job? About 80 percent of what you have to learn on this course is either ridiculous or not relevant,' said Frank Shaw, 67.

'I know how to greet a customer and lift a suitcase. I don't need a piece of paper to prove that.'

But Councillor Stephen Chappell, of the taxi licensing board, said: 'This qualification is vital.'

Daily Mirror 21/3/08

Xmas tree gets shield of steel

IT TRADITIONALLY takes pride of place in towns and villages where the mere sight of its twinkling lights spreads seasonal joy. But council bosses in one Scots village have taken the festive shine off their Christmas tree by surrounding it with a ring of steel to stop it from blowing over.

In a series of health and safety procedures that have stunned locals, not only have workers stuck the lush 10ft conifer in an unattractive concrete base, but they also placed heavy orange and white road barriers against it. And then, fearing that it was perhaps still not secure enough, they finally erected metal railings set in concrete bases to cage the tree off.

Fife Council said the measures were taken after the tree

on Anstruther seafront blew over several times last year. But locals of the east coast village say the council has taken the joy out of the tree and rendered it pointless.

They have taken to leaving messages on the fence – that bars them from even viewing the conifer properly, reading: 'Free the tree.'

Alan Stewart, 32, of the Christmas Tree Freedom Fighters campaign group, said: 'It's the most ridiculous looking tree I have ever seen. The measures to stop it falling are so over the top. The tree is only 10ft for goodness' sake. This is an insult to the people of Anstruther and an insult to the spirit of Christmas.'

George Miezitis, leader of the road services team which put up the tree, said the council felt the tree must be protected. 'The barriers against the tree base are a temporary measure which were put in place to protect the public when high winds were forecast. These will be removed, but the high fencing will remain.'

But locals insist the safety culture has now gone too far. 'The council's risk assessment team even took the weight of seagulls into account when coming up with these extreme measures,' said one.

Daily Mail 6/12/07

EU sinks carnival floats

CARNIVAL parades across Britain have been torpedoed by killjoy EU rules banning volunteer float drivers.

Haulage firms whose lorries have carried party platforms are pulling out as their drivers are banned from working for 45 hours after the events.

The truckers – many volunteering months in advance – now have to log private miles on tachographs in a bid to stop them from being overworked.

It means driving a float on a Saturday evening would ban them from getting behind the wheel again until Tuesday – leaving bosses in a pickle.

Bill Hockin, who has been giving 20 lorries to Devon's Barnstaple carnival for years, fears the law on drivers' hours may force him to stop. 'It's silly because the drivers love it and they find it relaxing. The men don't see it as work.'

The rule is a fresh blow to carnival bosses after new safety rules have forced them to tether anyone on a float to a harness. And directive EC 561/2006 has left at least two parades fearing for their largest floats.

Barnstaple may have to use smaller, tractor-pulled platforms or rely on walking entries – unless a solution is found soon.

Carnival marshal George Lovering, 68 – whose fete raises £3,000 each year – said: 'It would not be the same without the big floats.'

The Department of Transport said the EU rule is to improve road safety by ensuring drivers were less tired and could handle their HGVs better.

The Sun 21/3/08

Rink puts photos on ice

A FATHER says he is angry after being banned from taking photographs of his children skating on an ice rink.

Adrian Presbury, 43, of Oakwood, Derby, said staff told him it contravened the Child Protection Act and police would be called if he continued.

He was out with his son Thomas, 15, and daughter Lauren, five, at the city's new festive attraction in Market Place.

He was invited to pay £2 for photos taken by a professional photographer but said the ban had ruined his outing.

The rink's managers defended the action, saying Mr Presbury was breaching their health and safety policy because he was on the ice when he was taking the pictures.

Director of Derbyshire-based Creative Ice Chris Mullane said: 'He was told not to take photographs on the ice. That's very dangerous. He was taking photographs on the ice and breaking our rules and regulations.'

But Mr Presbury maintained that this was not the reason he was given at the time.

'I have got some sympathy with such a rule around places like swimming baths but when it's taking pictures of children wrapped up in balaclavas, coats and scarves it's political correctness gone mad.'

BBC News 12/12/07

Xmas comes early

CHRISTMAS comes but once a year – although in some areas it just happens to come much sooner than others. In Bury St Edmunds, Suffolk, the festive lights came on 80 days early because of health and safety checks.

Stunned visitors to the market town found themselves strolling beneath thousands of colourful bulbs a couple of weeks into autumn.

Chief critic of the £36,000 out-of-season display was Tory councillor Paul Hopfensperger – despite the fact his wife, Rebecca, is the town's mayor and chair of its Christmas lights committee.

'The whole town is in uproar. Everyone has been complaining to me about them,' he said. 'Not only are the lights up but they were on over the entire weekend.'

Others joining the chorus of disapproval included Bury Chamber of Commerce president Chrissie Harrod, who said: 'The lights should be saved until November 16 when they are switched on officially. I certainly wouldn't like to see Christmas starting any earlier than the six weeks we already have because people will get really fed up. Christmas gets earlier every year.'

But Mrs Hopfensperger blamed the early start on the need to safety test new lights and fittings. 'I'm well aware of everyone's concerns – including my husband's,' she said. 'But we must obey health and safety laws and have all the lights tested by both qualified electricians and Suffolk County Council.'

The council was criticised two years earlier when lights were banned from some buildings in case they set them ablaze. Days later health and safety zealots intervened again to switch off the lights on a huge Christmas tree in the town centre in case someone was electrocuted by the high-voltage cable running along the ground.

The fir tree was instead floodlit 'from a safe distance' and carol singers who traditionally gather around it were advised to bring torches to brighten up the scene.

dailymail.co.uk 10/10/06

Tighter trunks please

THREE lads were banned from a swimming pool because their trunks were not tight enough. They were told their knee-length shorts were banned because of health and safety rules.

Marc Smith, 13, brother Ryan, 12, and cousin Eliot Lee, also 12, were asked to change into 'appropriate' tight trunks or go home by an attendant at Harlow swimming pool, Essex.

Marc and Ryan's furious mum Amanda later rang the pool manager and was told their long shorts could hamper weaker swimmers.

Mrs Smith, 36, from Harlow, said: 'I had the manager tied up in knots. He said the drag of the material could impede swimming. Surely it comes down to how good a swimmer you are?

'Marc, Ryan and Eliot are all competent and my two are members of a swimming club.' She said that there had been no signs warning of the new policy.

The Sun 20/8/07

Fast firemen told to cool it

FIREMEN racing on 999 calls have been told to silence their sirens and drive within the speed limit because they pose a health and safety risk. Fire chiefs say the crews can only use their flashing lights and break the speed limit if there is an 'immediate' threat to life.

Outraged firemen in South Yorkshire have branded the new rules 'barmy' and say the safety measure could put more people's lives at risk.

One experienced fireman based in Sheffield said: 'Even if it seems to be a minor fire, you don't know how serious it really is until you get there. If we have to wait up to half an hour in traffic, it could have spread.'

The guidelines, issued to stations across South Yorkshire, say call-outs like skip blazes or car fires on 'dumping grounds' are examples of incidents when normal speeds and no sirens or lights should be used.

One firefighter based in Barnsley said: 'It's just barmy decision-making by pen-pushers who have no real knowledge of the job we do.'

Firemen have also been told that sirens, flashing lights and high speeds are banned for small or secondary fires, moorland fires, automatic fire alarm call-outs, minor flooding and people being stranded in lifts.

Tony Clay, head of operational standards and safety for South Yorkshire Fire and Rescue, said: 'We have all seen examples in the media of emergency vehicles being involved in road traffic collisions on the way to incidents. We are seeking to balance these equally important imperatives.'

Daily Express 19/6/07

No guard for May Queen

SCHOOL children have been banned from standing in a guard of honour at a town's annual May Fair celebrations – because it's too dangerous.

Parents of the children in Torrington, north Devon, have criticised the move after organisers of the traditional celebrations deemed the children would be at too much of a risk standing in a line holding bouquets.

In previous years all 200 children from Great Torrington's Bluecoat Infant and Nursery school have provided a guard of honour in the town square during the procession of the May Queen.

But now the town's May Fair committee and the head teachers of the infant and nursery school said there's a danger from over-crowding because a growing school population means there are too many children to fit in the square.

Parents have started a petition objecting to the ban saying it is a nail in the coffin of the town's May Day tradition.

One parent said: 'We understand there are health and safety issues but there has been no consultation – not even with the parents and friends group. This is a tradition and many parents are wondering what tradition will go next.'

But Infant school head teacher Mary Pearson said: 'Our priority is the children's safety. We have done a risk assessment and felt it was no longer safe for all the children to fit in the square.'

Mail on Sunday 5/4/07

School ban slammed

PARENTS have been banned from going inside a Cumbrian school building after a father who was hit by a door received £22,000 in compensation.

Peter Casson suffered facial injuries after he was hit by the door, which was caught by a gust of wind at St James Primary School, Millom.

A council spokesperson said it advises schools on health and safety issues but the decision to send the letter baring parents from the school had been made by the school and its governors.

In the letter, head teacher Maureen Hughes wrote: 'We must respectfully request that in future parents of children in junior classes remain outside the junior gates when collecting children from school. Parents will not be permitted to enter the school building.'

Parents and visitors who want to speak to a member of staff will have to do so by telephone.

BBC News 20/9/05

Pane in the arts

A BARMY council has banned local artists from displaying paintings behind glass – in case they fall and hurt somebody.

Another reason given was that someone might head-butt a picture and cut themselves. So works can no longer be hung at the library in traditional frames.

Ray Lovelock, of Flitwick Arts Society, Beds, said: 'It's health and safety gone mad. We were told that a painting could fall on someone – or a viewer could hurt themselves by head-butting the glass.'

But Bedfordshire County Councillor Bob King said: 'Paintings in glass frames are dangerous.'

The Sun 4/2/08

Killjoy cops block cup winners

HEALTH and safety concerns scuppered the homecoming parade for the newly crowned champions of European football, Manchester United.

Manchester will be the only city in recent memory not to

give a civic welcome home to their returning heroes, because police said it would risk public safety.

Earlier, in Portsmouth an estimated 150,000 lined the city's streets as the FA Cup winners returned home – there was one arrest. And when Liverpool won the European Cup in 2005 around one million welcomed the team home – again without major incident.

Despite widespread criticism and pleas from Manchester United's army of fans, Greater Manchester Police confirmed no homecoming parade would take place.

Assistant Chief Constable Dave Thompson said: 'It is right and fitting that MUFC's fans should have the chance to celebrate the club's success, but they should do this in safety.

'A review was carried out to assess the viability of an event and it was decided a parade could not take place because of the serious risk to public safety and major disruption to the rest of the community on a normal working and shopping day,' he added.

Defender Nemanja Vidic, 26, spoke for the team when he said: 'We're disappointed there is not going to be a victory parade. It would have been a good way to thank everyone for their support.'

Chester Standard 22/8/08

Thirsty flowers thwart council

FLOWER pots installed to cheer up Darlington's drab

ring road are to be removed – because of health and safety precautions. Every time the blooms have to be watered, one lane of traffic must be closed. Seven days' notice must also be given before any watering is carried out.

The line of planters were fixed to metal railings along the central reservation next to the roundabout at Northgate. When the flowers were in bloom the feature brightened up the concrete thoroughfare at one of Darlington's main access points.

Councillor Mark Burton noticed the flowers were wilting and got in touch with contractors Street Scene to report the problem.

'They were looking pretty limp, so I sent off an email to let them know they needed watering,' he said. 'That's when I found out they can't have them there any more and they need to be removed.'

A spokesperson for Darlington Borough Council confirmed the flowers had to go.

'It has been brought to our attention that to water these flowers would cause traffic problems, as this is a busy road which would have to be partially closed to allow a Street Scene team to work in the area,' she said. 'We have therefore decided to remove the flowers.

'Meanwhile, we are working with residents and community groups to make sure the borough is ready for the Northumbria in Bloom judges,' she added.

Northern Echo 16/5/08

Seat shifters for safety staff

IN MOST offices when a chair is in the wrong position then immediate action is taken. Somebody moves it. But not at the Health and Safety Executive.

There, employees have been banned from shifting furniture on the remote chance that they might do themselves a mischief.

They are told to book a porter to complete the task – and allow two days for it to happen. The new rule could prove particularly problematic for staff planning a last-minute meeting.

If a porter cannot be summoned urgently staff would be left with the awkward choice of disobeying a direct order from the management or asking some of their guests to stand.

To hammer home the point, signs which read: 'Do not lift tables or chairs without giving 48 hours notice to HSE management', have been plastered across the walls in several meeting rooms.

Labour peer Lord Berkeley noticed the signs on a visit to HSE HQ. 'It's ridiculous to mollycoddle people like that. It's taking health and safety precautions to a ridiculous level. They ought to be concentrating on the important things.

'The HSE is an office like any other – so if it is not required in other offices, why there? It's the epitome of a nanny state.'

Lord Berkeley also criticised the HSE for sending home staff from a meeting he was attending after it had snowed. 'We were told we had to go home because there was an inch of snow on the ground outside,' he said. 'The buses and trains were still running. It's just preposterous.'

The signs have been put up in almost all of the 31 HSE

offices across the country, where 3,600 staff are employed.

A spokesperson said: 'HSE's approach to moving furniture in its offices is based on its own assessment of the risks from manual handling – one of the main causes of work-related absence among its staff.'

Daily Mail 2/4/07

Shoo your own gulls says council

A SEMI-retired driving instructor said he was lost for words after a council employee suggested he climb onto a neighbour's roof to deal with the problem of noisy, messy seagulls which were causing him a nuisance.

Peter Finalyson said he called the environmental services department at Moray Council headquarters in Elgin to report the noisy birds, which are busy nesting and creating a disturbance.

Mr Finlayson said he received very little help and was told he would have to sort the problem himself.

'When I told the woman at the council about the problem and asked her what I should do, she said they couldn't help,' said Mr Finlayson. 'She said I should sort them out myself. I couldn't believe it. I was so angry.'

'We are aware of the various problems caused by gulls and sympathise with those affected,' said a council spokesperson. 'However, it is the responsibility of the owner of the dwelling to proof their property and prevent gulls nesting.'

'So much for health and safety,' said Mr Finalyson. 'Imagine telling a pensioner to climb up on a roof. I asked who would be liable should I slip on their roof and take out some slates. There was no answer to that.'

Forres Gazette 30/4/08

Don't go to work on an egg

FIFTY years after Britons were implored to 'Go to work on an egg', an advertising watchdog has banned a revival of the campaign, saying that it breaches health guidelines.

Plans to mark the anniversary by broadcasting the original television advertisements featuring Tony Hancock have had to be called off.

The ban by the Broadcast Advertising Clearance Centre, which vets television advertisements, was condemned as ridiculous by the novelist Fay Weldon, who used to work in advertising and helped to create the campaign.

'I think the ruling is absurd,' she said. 'We seem to have been tainted by all the health and safety laws. If they are going to ban egg adverts then I think they should ban all car adverts, because cars really are dangerous, and bad for the environment.'

The advertising clearance centre, a government-backed watchdog, says that it blocked the campaign because eating an egg for breakfast every day was not a 'varied diet'.

The egg information service said it was shocked by the ruling. It said eggs are a healthy food recommended by nutritionists and many other advertisers promote their products to be eaten every day, 'so we are very surprised eggs have been singled out'.

'There are no restrictions on the number of eggs people can eat, which was recently confirmed by the Food Standards Agency, and between five and seven eggs a week would be totally acceptable for most people,' it said in a statement.

The advertising clearance centre stood by its ban, saying: 'Dietary considerations have been at the centre of the new rules for advertising and we felt these ads did not suggest a varied diet.'

The Times 20/6/07

Off your bike

HUNDREDS of police officers in Greater Manchester have been banned from patrolling on their bicycles on health and safety grounds.

The move follows the death of a Police Community Support Officer who was on duty when his bicycle was hit by a lorry in Hindley Green, Wigan.

All officers with less than a year's experience on a bike have now been stopped while a review is carried out. Other officers will be given extra safety advice.

A spokesperson said: 'Following consultation with our health and safety training unit and Unison, we feel confident that officers who have patrolled on bikes for more than 12 months have sufficient experience and road awareness to continue to ride.

'They will be given supplementary advice regarding the Highway Code and safe riding and we will support anybody who has concerns about continuing to patrol on their bikes.

'We hope the officers affected by this review will be back patrolling on bikes in a couple of months.'

BBC News 24/9/07

Brussels tests go down a bomb

FIREWORK displays from the largest Guy Fawkes Night spectacle to the smallest back-garden show are under threat from new European legislation.

A directive approved by MEPs and EU ministers will force Britain and other member nations to tear up their own safety standards and adopt new regulations by 2010.

Health and safety bureaucrats in Brussels also want to make manufacturers pay for the re-testing of tens of thousands of fireworks already considered safe in Britain.

Tom Smith, the Confederation of British Industry spokesman for pyrotechnics, said: 'Not a single person in Britain will be made safer by all this additional testing, but everyone will be affected by it becoming much more expensive and bureaucratic,' he said.

'It's a very real threat. We wouldn't even have a display at the opening ceremony of the London Olympics.'

As part of the change, people will be told to retire at

least 26ft after lighting a firework, as opposed to the current 16ft – effectively ruling out many displays at home.

Tom Smith added: 'Many people will no longer be able to use fireworks as they haven't got 26ft of space in their gardens.'

Daily Mail 16/2/08

Cruisers blast overboard safety tests

IT WAS a case of health and safety gone mad when 'bin day' took on a whole new meaning for volunteers from the Surrey and Hampshire Canal Society.

The volunteers were forced to come up with a creative way to simulate 50 passengers on a canal boat for a Marine and Coastguard Agency (MCA) safety test.

Using real people was ruled out under health and safety regulations.

The volunteers, mainly retired locals, used bins filled with water to test whether their canal boat, *The John Pinkerton*, could safely carry 50 passengers if they all moved to one side of the boat.

Earlier plans to use soldiers from the nearby Pirbright Camp were over-ruled on the same safety grounds.

But critics argue the tests are overly stringent. The boat operates at a maximum speed of 3mph on a canal where the maximum depth is 3ft 6in and the maximum flow is less than 1mph.

'The maximum wave height even in hurricane winds is

one inch and no icebergs have been sighted for at least 30 years,' said Nigel Bird of Surrey and Hampshire Canal Cruises. 'Our boat operates on a static canal and still has to comply with the same rules as boats on the Thames which have to deal with currents and tides.'

Surrey Hants Star 8/5/08

Schools ponder hot tea fear

SCHOOLS could be told to stop serving hot tea to under 16s on health and safety grounds.

The government-funded School Food Trust said restrictions may be added to guidelines on drinks approved for consumption in State schools.

In a consultation document, it said hot coffee and tea had 'minimal' nutritional benefits and posed potential safety risks.

Draft guidelines – part of a drive to improve the quality of food served in schools – say any drinks served in schools in addition to water 'should offer clear nutritional benefit'.

It said allowing hot tea, coffee and low-calorie hot chocolate were 'obvious inconsistencies'.

Mick Brookes, the general secretary of the National Association of Head Teachers, said: 'I can understand the anxiety about young people eating appropriate food but this nannying really has to end. This just cuts into people's civil liberties.'

Daily Telegraph 17/2/08

Bike ban prompts fun day flop

COUNCIL chiefs have come under fire after banning a church from staging quad bike rides as part of a family fun day.

Totton and Eling Town Council has imposed the ban because it fears it could be prosecuted if someone was killed or seriously injured in an accident.

Members took the decision after hearing that Testwood Baptist Church had applied to stage the rides on council-owned land.

However, former council chairman David Harrison spoke in favour of quad bike rides. 'I'm struggling to imagine what would make us liable if there was an accident,' he said. 'We're talking about a very small area that will be fenced off for vehicles that won't be travelling at great speed.'

John Cunningham, one of the organisers, said: 'We have staged quad bikes rides for the past two years and haven't had any problems. They're a big draw and obviously we're disappointed we won't be able to stage them again this year.'

But council chairman Di Brooks blamed the need for insurance. 'The government says quad bike rides needs to be licensed and gave us a list of about ten organisations but none of them could help. They're more into on-road events.'

Southern Daily Echo 2/5/08

Off your balls

IF ANYONE knows about sitting comfortably – and safely – at work it is a team of university physiotherapists. That's why staff at Bath University began using giant inflatable balls as office chairs.

The rubber Swiss balls, developed in the 1970s as an exercise aide, are a recognised method of strengthening the muscles that support the back. But their health and safety initiative soon fell foul of health and safety officials.

They said staff could fall off the balls or the inflatables could roll around the office and hurt someone. The physios were advised to go back to chairs.

But top physiotherapist Sonya Crowe, one of about half a dozen staff using the balls as chairs, has no intention of complying. She insists that any risk is minimal.

'I've never heard of anyone falling off one of the balls,' she said. 'The health benefits far outweigh any risks there may be.'

She was backed by the Chartered Society of Physiotherapy which said: 'There's absolutely no risk with these things if they are used properly. The health and safety people need to remember that not all chairs have four legs.'

A spokesperson for Bath University, which offers one of the UK's best degree courses in sport and exercise science, said health and safety officials were now thinking again.

'The health and safety department advised us that the

exercise balls don't fit in with the health and safety policy. They just don't feel people should be using them and asked them to stop.'

This is London 11/5/07

Knitting needles safety managers

A HOSPITAL has removed a box of wool and knitting needles from public access, claiming it was a safety hazard.

For three years, the Congleton War Memorial Hospital in Cheshire had provided a knitting box in its main waiting area, containing wool and needles, and invited patients and visitors to knit a square while they waited.

In that time, there had not been a single accident, injury or complaint. But health and safety staff at the small community hospital decided the box had to go in case someone got hurt.

The chairman of the League of Friends, Michael Lambert, said: 'The idea was you would knit a small square and they were all sent off to charities and turned into large blankets and clothes for the needy. The knitting box was extremely popular and now it has been taken away.'

Knitting groups branded the ban 'daft'. Martine de Lee, chairman of the UK Knitting and Crochet Guild, said: 'This is ridiculous. If it wasn't so sad I would laugh. This policy needs to be looked at again.'

However, the East Cheshire NHS Trust defended its action and said it was trying to create a safe environment for patients.

Bernie Salisbury, director of nursing and operations, said: 'We were concerned about the ease with which youngsters could access knitting needles in the waiting area and believe this sensible and pro-active measure will avoid preventable accidents. The box has now been placed behind the hospital's main reception desk and is available on request.'

Daily Telegraph 17/9/07

Dancers blast ballroom carpet

YOU WON'T catch the professionals from Strictly Come Dancing attempting to display their moves on a patch of carpet. But that could be the fate of amateur dancers in Blackpool after their traditional shiny floors fell foul of health and safety experts.

The dance floors are all being carpeted over because the local council says the risk of people slipping over on them is too great.

It admits that this has scuppered the dancers, but claims the non-slip surface is more suitable for other activities – such as karate.

Baffled locals said they could not remember anyone hurting themselves on the floors and accused bureaucrats of showing a lack of common sense.

Doreen Holt, a councillor who uses Ibbison Court community centre, said: 'It's such a shame because it was a good, gentle form of exercise for them, and we're always being told how we need to be more active these days.

'Now the worry is that the same thing will happen at the school and they'll have nowhere to go.'

The move is part of Blackpool council's £250,000 upgrade of 16 community centres to bring them in line with disability guidelines. A spokesperson said smooth, slippery floors had been deemed unsuitable for the pensioners who form a large proportion of the centres' users.

They also made the venues warmer and more comfortable and meant spillages were easier to clean up.

Among the dance enthusiasts forced to move elsewhere is 72-year-old Edwina Parker, who ran the group at Ibbison Court.

'We're very disappointed,' she said. 'We used to enjoy our dances there, it made you feel ten years younger, and we're sorry it's come to an end. But that's health and safety, I suppose.'

Daily Mail 4/2/08

Jolly panto rogered

A SWASHBUCKLING amateur dramatics group has been ordered by health and safety bosses to keep its toy plastic swords under lock and key when not in use on stage.

The village theatre company has had to promise to guard the toy cutlasses used in its pantomime, *Robinson Crusoe*.

Actors have also been told that the props – including

plastic spears and toy gun which fires a flag with the word 'bang' – are classed as replica weapons. And officials have also warned the Carnon Downs Drama Group that risk assessments should be carried out on frying pans used in stage fights.

Director Linda Barker said: 'In some scenes, pirates are hitting each other with frying pans and saucepan lids, but there's no problem with them. We've got several wooden and plastic swords, two plastic spears and a gun which cost £2 from a joke shop. But now we need to keep them locked away and fill out all sorts of forms.'

The group first realised it had to register the props after being alerted by the National Operatic and Dramatic Association to new legislation on the use of weapons or their replicas in productions.

Elaine Gummow, co-director of the panto, said: 'There was an article in a recent magazine about the use of weapons in productions. It told members they had to carry out a full-risk assessment and follow new health and safety guidelines if any weapons, including replica weapons, are used on stage.'

The group's version of *Robinson Crusoe* is a traditional village panto with a Cornish flavour and is set in Falmouth harbour. 'It all seems a bit absurd but it is perhaps a sign of the times – health and safety is everywhere,' said Ms Gummow.

The group informed the police it had no malicious intent and planned to use the weapons in its show – but was then told by police it must also inform the fire brigade.

Neighbourhood beat officer PC Nigel Hyde said: 'I gather we've made a note and it seems a bit unusual. But other forms of replica weapons have been used to carry out crimes and the consequences have been serious.'

Western Morning News 18/1/08

Walkers forced to drive to dump

HEALTH and safety rules stopped a Kidderminster couple from walking through the gate of the Hoobrook household waste tip carrying four bags of rubbish.

Retired railway signal designer, Richard Rathbone, 62, described the regulation as 'idiotic' and blasted health and safety precautions for reaching 'ludicrous levels'.

He and his wife, Barbara, 68, walked to the tip but were told they could not walk through the gate, even though they could walk freely around the site after they had driven in.

Mr Rathbone had to go back for his car, drive to the gate, pick up his wife, load the bags and drive through the gate to deposit his garden waste and Tetra Pak drinks cartons.

'We could walk up to the gate, we could walk around on the other side of the gate, but we could not walk the two steps through the gate. It just struck us as being a total nonsense.'

A Worcestershire County Council spokesperson said: 'It is county council policy not to allow people to enter the waste sites on foot.

'There are health and safety issues surrounding this that mean people cannot walk though the gates with their rubbish into the waste sites.

'The county council takes people's safety very seriously

and policies are put into place to protect them from harm,' he added.

Kidderminster Shuttle 9/5/08

Don't feed danger ducks

THE AGE-OLD tradition of feeding the ducks has been banned at a picturesque village pond – because councillors fear bird droppings could harm children and pollute the pond.

Official signs have been put up to remind any disobedient duck feeders the activity is now officially banned at the 400-year-old pond in Oakley, near Basingstoke, Hants.

Oakley and Deane Parish Council admits it has little proof to back up the fears but denied it was overreacting.

Chairperson John Strawbridge said: 'The pond has always been popular with locals and an attractive feature of Oakley. But the duck population has increased dramatically and their droppings are starting to pollute the pond and the neighbouring area.

'We don't want to be killjoys and we'd like to encourage people to carry on enjoying it, but feeding the ducks puts a strain on its entire eco-system.'

Parish council vice chairman Margaret Burgess, 67, insisted her four grandchildren would no longer be feeding the birds. 'Bread is not good for the ducks' digestive systems and we think the excess droppings may be harmful and spread diseases. I don't know there's particular proof but that's the concern.'

However, villager Hilary Box, 75, who had a contract for 22 years to feed the ducks, described the ban as sad and symptomatic of a 'nanny state' culture.

'The sign says that feeding bread to ducks can be bad for them but I think we have the healthiest ducks in the world,' she said. 'The bread does not appear to have done them any harm and they haven't suffered over the years. Feeding ducks is part of the English way of life.'

Daily Mail 25/10/07

Ring ban blow to swimmers

A COUNCIL has banned its leisure centres from lending rubber rings and armbands to swimmers amid health and safety fears.

Blowing up the inflatables by mouth is considered too risky for spreading germs and unseen punctures might lead to an accident.

Bournemouth Borough Council in Dorset has imposed the ban following professional guidelines from the Institute of Sport and Recreation Management.

The ban comes after an auditor spotted one of the swimming pools lending out armbands. Parents and staff have branded it a blow against common sense.

One father said: 'Yes, there are germs when different

people inflate the same arm bands and rubber-rings but the time-honoured practice of mums and dads blowing these up – much to the excitement of toddlers – has been going on for decades, without people keeling over from contagious illnesses.'

Bournemouth Daily Echo 22/7/07

Council ban bananas

A GREENGROCER has been told to remove his veg stall – in case someone slips on a banana.

For 20 years Steve Taylor has displayed produce outside his shop in Bacup Road, Waterfoot. But now town hall officials say it poses a health and safety hazard.

Steve's shop is next to a 12ft-wide pavement, which he said allows shoppers plenty of space to pass his 2ft-wide table. In 20 years, there has never been an accident.

But planners at Lancashire County Council sent him a letter saying it is illegal for traders to obstruct a public highway. They told him any accidents would be the liability of the shopkeeper.

Father-of-six Steve, 50, said: 'It's bananas. I was warned about this more than 10 years ago but the council agreed commonsense should prevail.

'Everyone says that the display brightens up the street and brings a bit of character to the area, but the council just wants everything to look the same.'

Salford Advertiser 28/9/07

Red noses blown

RED NOSES have been banned from the set of the BBC's celebrity Fame Academy special – even though it is raising funds for Comic Relief – because they have been deemed a fire risk.

A spokesperson for producers Endemol said: 'We have to comply with health and safety rules. It's not just red noses, it's papers, bottles and bags as well.'

All non-essential items are banned from the studio areas of the Grade II-listed County Hall in central London where the programme is being filmed.

BBC News 13/3/07

Lap lessons for Santa

FATHER Christmases working in shopping centre grottos are receiving special training to ensure they do not injure themselves while perching children on their knees.

Environmental health officials have introduced training courses for Santas to help them avoid back ache during their present-giving duties.

The classes include advice on the correct posture Santas should adopt in their chairs as youngsters announce their Christmas wish lists.

They are also being instructed on the best methods to lift heavy gifts from under the tree to prevent doing themselves an injury.

The Chartered Institute of Environmental Health says Santas do not possess any magical immunity from work-related injuries.

Daily Telegraph 5/12/08

Warning weeder at work

JUNE Turnbull, 79, has been looking after the flora and fauna in the village of Urchfont in Wiltshire since 1999 out of the goodness of her heart. She even has to fork out for flowers and compost from her pension.

But now council officials have ordered her to leave her labour of love – or comply with health and safety regulations.

From now on she must wear a fluorescent safety jacket and surround herself with three metal warning signs.

But June has chosen to defy the council's demands, saying she is physically unable to drag three metal signs around with her. She loves doing her gardening so much that she intends to continue – even if it means going to jail.

Wiltshire county council made their demands after they

were alerted by a highway inspector who had seen June hard at work weeding.

He asked the village's parish council if they had the necessary safety license for her, and told them they had health and safety responsibility for volunteers on county-owned land.

Parish council chairman, Peter Newell, said: 'She has done a wonderful job for the past eight years. We all think the council is going a bit over the top.'

The One Show, BBC 10/8/07

Talc targeted as slip risk

A BAN on talcum powder and air fresheners on hospital wards – because they might cause patients to slip and fall – has been attacked as 'ludicrous' by the campaigner fronting the appeal to Save Bridlington Hospital.

Mick Pilling said threats of closure and staff shortages were the main issues at the East Yorkshire hospital and the ban on the products was silly.

'What will be next?' he asked. 'No fruit in case any peel goes on the floor? I think the ban is a ludicrous decision. Patients need to use aerosols to keep clean and talc to stop irritations caused by sitting on a bed all the time.'

He insisted that hospital chiefs should concentrate on more serious matters. 'The main issue at the moment is the shortage of nurses, they are working flat out, but hospital chiefs come up with these silly ideas and don't look at the main issues,' he added.

Sue Wellington, manager at Bridlington Hospital, put up posters around the wards saying the ban was 'a result of advice from the Health and Safety Executive'.

The executive, however, insists it has not told any hospitals to ban the products.

A spokesperson for the hospital health trust said: 'People may think this sounds like bureaucracy but it's simple common sense in the face of a very important issue.

'In particular, if talc gets on to the soles of slippers, a fall is more likely, hence the decision to ask people not to use it,' he said. 'Any inconvenience in not using talc is far outweighed by the safety angle which is really good common sense, and is something that people might like to bear in mind if they have vinyl floors in their own bathrooms.'

Yorkshire Post 12/3/07

School bans danger ties

A SCHOOL has banned pupils from wearing ties to class in a bid to prevent serious injuries.

Teachers at Bramhall High School in Stockport sent out letters ordering pupils to leave their ties at home and replace them with clip-on versions. They argue knotted ties can pose a health and safety risk and told the 1,500 pupils to use the safer clip-on versions or face being sent home.

The school says activities such as science and woodwork,

where heavy machinery and naked flames are commonplace, could lead to pupils sustaining serious injuries because of trailing ties.

Head teacher John Peckham said the new policy was a sensible measure. 'We have been only selling clip-on ties for more than a year in an effort to phase this in but we are now at the stage where older pupils are wearing old and dirty ties because they don't want to replace them.

'Obviously there is a health and safety element. Pupils can take precautions during technical lessons where there is machinery but it is the unexpected factors such as running and having their ties pulled that could be a problem.'

The parent of a 15-year-old pupil said: 'There has always been a strong uniform policy, which I have supported, but I think this is very silly. Where is this health and safety thing going to end? I have never heard of a school going this far before.'

Nick Seaton, chair of the Campaign for Real Education, said the decision was inexplicable. 'It seems like another instance of political correctness and health and safety gone mad. Children have worn school ties for decades and I have never heard of an accident in all that time.'

Manchester Evening News 17/3/07

Hard to swallow

MINCE pies have been banned from a primary school's Christmas fete over fears they could be a health and safety hazard with pupils suffering adverse reactions to some of the ingredients.

Neil Davies, head teacher at Mynydd Cynffig Junior School in Kenfig Hill, near Porthcawl, said: 'I have got to guarantee the health and safety of the pupils. I'm not doing it to upset anybody.'

But his decision has upset some parents who argue home-cooked food is often the healthier option and is, after all, what most of the children eat at home.

Bridgend County Borough Council's cabinet member for education, Peter Foley, branded the decision an over-reaction. 'Children are going to be gorging themselves on home-made products in the Christmas season and I see no harm in them being on sale,' he said.

One mother whose son attends the school said: 'It seems crazy – we invite our children's friends round for parties at home and serve up mince pies we've cooked, so what's the difference selling them at the school Christmas fair?'

Daily Telegraph 3/12/07

Killjoys lick festive lollipop lady

A LOLLIPOP lady who has put on festive fancy dress for the past 20 years has been banned from spreading Christmas cheer by Scrooge-like council chiefs.

Margaret Russell, 54, has delighted pupils, their parents and passing motorists in Millbrook for two decades with her festive costumes to raise money for charity.

In previous years she has helped children cross the road dressed as a turkey, a reindeer, a star and even a Christmas tree. But following a complaint by two parents the council said she could not dress up.

Margaret, of Chiltern Green, Millbrook, who is collecting for the Mayor of Southampton's appeal fund, said: 'I'm a bit disappointed and I think there will be a lot of people who miss my costumes as well.'

Over the years Margaret has raised thousands of pounds for charity but is not expecting to raise as much this year in her normal uniform.

The latest home-made costume, a large golden bell, took Margaret a month to make and was designed so she could give herself a big send off after 20 years of fundraising.

A spokesperson for Southampton City Council said: 'Mrs Russell could not have carried out her usual crossing duties because she wasn't wearing her reflective clothing which is against the law.

'If a crossing patrol supervisor does not wear a reflective jacket they are not insured and if hit, the motorist could not be prosecuted.'

Millbrook ward councillor Ceren Davis said Margaret should be allowed to wear her festive gear. 'It seems these days that the council is frightened of people suing them. If nothing has happened over the years why would it happen now?'

Southern Daily Echo 11/12/07

Incoming mortars

STUDENTS have been asked not to throw their hats in the air when they graduate because it is too dangerous.

Anglia Ruskin University, which has campuses in Cambridge and Chelmsford, Essex, does not want graduates to throw their mortar boards into the sky in case the corner of the hat injures someone.

The request was made in a statement on the university's website.

Alongside details about which robes students should wear at graduation ceremonies, the statement reads: 'It is requested that graduates do not throw their hats up into the air.

'This not only causes damage to the hats but it can also cause injury if the corner of the hat hits graduates or others who may be nearby.'

The Sun 28/5/08

Pancakes hit safety hurdle

A SHROVETIDE pancake race due to be staged in Ripon as part of celebrations going back 600 years has been abandoned because of hurdles imposed by local health and safety officials.

A pancake bell on Ripon Cathedral has been rung at 11am on Shrove Tuesday since the 15thCentury to warn people to use up their left-over eggs and flour before the start of the Lent fast – the origins of pancake day.

For the past 11 years, it has also marked the start of a pancake race which revived traditions going back almost as long.

Now the event has been cancelled because of demands made by health and safety, insurance companies and new rules under which police and the local council can charge for the expense of closing down streets.

'It was the health and safety regulations which were the last straw,' says the Dean of Ripon, the Very Rev. Keith Jukes. 'There are so many forms to fill in that volunteers who organised and marshalled the race in the past gave up.'

One of the organisers, Councillor Bernard Batemen, complained: 'The paper work which started out as well-meaning has now gone overboard. It puts people off helping.'

Yorkshire Dales Country News 5/2/08

Cleaners grounded in pipe ban

THE livelihoods of hundreds of thousands of window cleaners could be threatened by a tough new hosepipe law. Under a government proposal to tackle future droughts, it would be illegal to use hosepipes for a number of activities from filling swimming pools to cleaning windows.

Up to half the nation's estimated 400,000 window cleaners have recently dispensed with the traditional bucket and sponge to placate health and safety officials in favour of a ladder-free system of poles which relies on hosepipes.

Andrew Lee, vice-chairman of the Federation for Window Cleaners, said: 'It's going to be disastrous if we are included in the ban. I can't encourage people to break the law but that's what these boys are going to be faced with.'

The concern follows moves by the government to update the 62-year-old drought legislation, which only restricts the use of hosepipes for watering gardens and washing cars. The new law would allow water companies to enforce a 'discretionary use' ban, outlawing virtually all domestic activities involving hosepipes.

Window cleaners, under pressure from health and safety legislation which discourages the use of ladders, have been converting their businesses to water-fed poles.

However, a spokesperson for the Department for Environment Food and Rural Affairs confirmed that water-fed poles would be covered by a hosepipe ban under the law. 'Window cleaners could still revert to a bucket and sponge.'

Daily Telegraph 23/10/07

Stress strikes HSE staff

THEY ARE the ones who lecture bosses on how to protect workers from stress. But the job seems to be too much for the health and safety experts themselves as droves are taking time off – with stress.

Hundreds of officials are calling in sick, leaving

taxpayers to foot the bill.

The Health and Safety Executive (HSE) has admitted that more than one in five sick days taken by its staff is blamed on stress.

The cost runs to more than £500,000 a year for those missing with stress and almost the same again for absences with 'symptoms ill defined'.

The problem has become so bad that the HSE has started a drive to cut the amount of time taken off, particularly by women. The campaign appears to be based on encouraging managers to take a tougher line with workers pleading stress.

A report prepared for the organisation added that 'many feel the HSE's management of stress is inadequate'.

But some business leaders say health and safety inspectors should examine their own troubles before lecturing others. Stephen Alambritis, of the Federation of Small Businesses, said: 'They have been hoisted by their own petard.'

In total, more than five million working days are lost in Britain each year to complaints of stress. The HSE has told firms to treat it as seriously as industrial accidents and injuries.

Daily Mail 7/3/08

Bill for bloom baskets

ITS' beautiful blooms and colourful floral displays have

delighted visitors for the last 12 years but now the award-winning village of Filby near Yarmouth has become the latest victim of stringent health and safety rules after being told it can no longer decorate lamp posts with hanging baskets.

Organisers of the successful Filby in Bloom event have been told by Yarmouth Borough Council they can not put flower-filled baskets on about 60 lamp posts because the old off-street lighting columns could fall over because of the added weight.

The council fears that if a crumbling lamp post toppled over and injured or killed someone, the authority could be sued for negligence.

Filby in Bloom, which has clinched the title of East Anglian's best kept village for the last 10 years, has been told that it may also have to contribute £9,000 to the town's new lamp posts so they can take the weight of the 40lb baskets.

'We are disappointed by this news and it may have an affect on the judges,' said event organiser Adrian Thompson. 'In the last 12 years, we never had a health and safety issue over the lamp posts. The only problem we have had is when a yob pulled one down.'

Simon Mutten, council environmental services manager, said: 'A risk has been bought to our attention by professionals and we cannot ignore it because if we did and something, however unlikely, happened then we would be taken to the cleaners.'

Eastern Daily Press 10/1/08

Convicts go under cover

CONVICTED criminals working in the community are to be barred from wearing fluorescent jackets because their feelings might be hurt if passers-by hurl abuse.

Government officials are also worried about the health and safety of burglars and thugs if they can be identified while they carry out their punishments.

In a spectacular U-turn, probation staff have been told to stop putting up signs saying street work is being carried out by convicts – or forcing them to wear bright yellow jackets branded 'Community Payback'.

Instead, a small plaque will be erected long after the yobs have gone to make sure their delicate sensibilities are not put at risk. The decision makes a mockery of repeated New Labour promises to make 'tough' community sentences – such as tidying parks and fixing benches – more visible so that the public can see justice being done.

Probation note PC30/2007, titled Health and Safety Considerations When Delivering Unpaid Work, says: 'There have been some instances of offenders and unpaid work staff being abused or attacked whilst on unpaid work sites. Local managers have a responsibility for the safety of staff and offenders engaged in unpaid work and must take this into account when deciding which sites to badge as Community Payback.'

The Ministry of Justice is obliged to consider the health and safety of the criminals as, technically, it is their employer.

In a classic example of Whitehall confusion, some criminals working in the open air will still wear the bright yellow jackets but without any logo to suggest they are convicts.

Why? Because the high-visibility jackets could help prevent accidents – as required under health and safety rules.

London Lite 10/9/07

Police see red over Xmas lights

A FESTIVE cleaner was shocked when police pulled her over – for having a red bulb on her in-car Christmas lights.

For the past four years Michelle Lea, 32, of Abbotsbury Road, Weymouth, has put festive lights on her dashboard. But police say she must replace the red bulb with another colour because red is an 'offence'.

'I think it's pathetic. To get two points and fine for a tiny red light! The lights are hardly dazzling. You can buy these lights all over the place. What are the police going to do? Remove them from all the shops?'

But Dorset Police denied being Christmas killjoys – claiming safety must come first. 'You're not allowed to display red lights to the front of any vehicle and our advice is not to display any Christmas decorations in your vehicle as they can distract the driver and confuse other road users.

'One of the problems is that brake lights are red – so someone in front could think they are looking at the back end of a vehicle when they are looking at the front.'

Michelle added: 'I don't think I'll be using the lights again – even the ones that aren't red. It's not worth the hassle. But there'll be a little less festive cheer in my car this year.'

Dorset Echo 12/12/06

Stop, mourners crossing

ELECTRIC golf buggies could be used by disabled people to get around a cemetery following a ban on cars. Wrexham Council say they have no choice but to ban all cars for health and safety reasons.

Disabled campaigners in the town have criticised the car ban. 'I think it's ludicrous,' said Harry Prankard, chairman of Wrexham Disability Forum. 'They're going to stop all cars going in there saying people could get run over. I've never heard of anyone getting run over in a graveyard.'

However, an internal council auditor who monitored the use of cars in Wrexham Cemetery, noticed serious problems.

'During our inspection a party of walkers, including a disabled visitor using crutches, had to give way to a vehicle requiring access and, as a result, had to climb on top of gravestones adjacent to the roadway,' he said.

Wrexham Council has increased exclusive parking bays for disabled visitors and placed extra benches for them to sit on to reduce the distance they walk.

A feasibility study will be carried out to investigate the possibility of introducing another form of transport like golf buggies for disabled visitors.

BBC News 23/3/04

Flight ban crackers

HOLIDAY travellers will not be allowed to take Christmas crackers on planes for security reasons.

Staff at Stansted airport in Essex said dangerous items might be hidden inside and crackers could frighten other passengers if they went bang.

A spokesperson said: 'We won't allow them in hand luggage, basically because we can't see what's inside.

'We would have to take them apart and that would defeat the object. And most airlines don't want crackers in packed luggage. A bang from a cracker could cause alarm on a plane. Our message is don't bring Christmas crackers if you're flying over the holiday period.'

Channel 4 News 18/12/07

Bath towel test slips up

IT IS not a problem that springs readily to mind – unless perhaps you are about to step dripping wet out of the bath. Even then, the question of whether or not to put a towel on the floor would be a fleeting one at best, especially if you have already invested in a bath mat.

But researchers investigating 'The Role of Towels As A Control to Reduce Slip Potential' are wringing out every drop of information on the topic.

They have spent close to a month and £12,000 of taxpayers' money trying to find out whether a towel on a bathroom floor makes one less likely to slip.

The study, carried out for the Health and Safety Executive, involved researchers squeezing varying amounts of water on a variety of different floor surfaces.

The team, based at the Health and Safety Laboratory in Buxton, Derbyshire, bought a set of identical towels from a local supermarket. They splashed rough tiles and smooth tiles and worn vinyl and new vinyl with varying amounts of water.

Then, using a machine-operated pendulum, they measured the friction produced from a towel rubbing against the surfaces.

'Unfortunately, the testing carried out here is insufficient to draw significant conclusions,' their report admitted.

Kevin Hallas, who lead the investigation, said: 'We expected the investigation to be more straightforward than it was. We need to do more work.'

Evening Standard 4/8/07

Minister in tinsel alert

THE government has issued safety guidelines to help

families survive Christmas with warnings that children could be hurt if they fall off rocking horses or ride their new bikes into walls.

The Department for Children, Schools and Families has printed the 150,000 leaflets designed to look like advent calendars 'to help make the festive season safe'.

The leaflets alert parents to the dangers of tinsel, with a thousand people each year apparently 'hurt by trimmings or when decorating their homes'.

Safety tips featured in *Tis the Season to be Careful* include a warning that parents may cut themselves with knives when trying to open presents and that baubles can break easily.

Children's minister Delyth Morgan says the leaflets will help 'make sure Christmas is a time for fun and laughter but not tears'.

Tory junior children's spokesman Tim Loughton said: 'It's ironic that a government department which has become accident prone for messing up test results, pouring millions into databases that don't work and failing to protect our most vulnerable children is now spending thousands on producing leaflets to state the blindingly obvious.'

Daily Telegraph 22/12/08

Don't fetch, Fido

A TOP vet is warning that dogs suffer as many injuries chasing and catching sticks as they do on Britain's roads. Owners should never throw sticks if they want to avoid an accidental stabbing or choking – they should use rubber toys instead.

'When I see people throwing sticks for their dogs in the park I just get so frustrated,' says Dan Brockman, professor of small animal surgery at the Royal Veterinary College. 'I want to go and tell them to stop.'

Professor Brockman says it's not just the dogs that suffer. 'I have seen injuries that have cost up to £5,000 in treatment fees – but where the dog has still died in the end.'

He also cautions that people who get their pets to fetch balls may also be behaving irresponsibly.

'You must make sure the size of ball is right for the dog,' he said. 'I have had to operate on dogs that have swallowed tennis balls too.'

The Times 28/12/08

Nut boy in school ban

A BOY with a severe nut allergy has been banned from his school because his teachers say he is a health and safety risk.

Four days after starting his new secondary school, George Hall-Lambert's mother Judith was told to remove him after his allergy came to light.

She said: 'I am absolutely appalled. It's a shambles. The school should be able to deal with children like George. He is being discriminated against because he has a nut allergy. He's a bright kid and this could really set back his education.'

The 11-year-old carries an emergency adrenaline

injection – an EpiPen – and wears a medical tag to alert people to his condition.

His mother informed Howden School in East Yorkshire of his allergy before the term began. The comprehensive school has now offered to allow George to return in its special needs unit, but Mrs Hall-Lambert has refused.

'George is well-behaved and there is no reason for him to be in that unit. He is entitled to a mainstream education like everyone else,' she explained.

Head teacher Andrew Williams said: 'We're working with everyone to reach a solution.'

But a spokesperson for the Anaphylaxis Campaign said: 'This is way out of the ordinary.'

Sky News 28/9/07

Silent night for hospital choir

CAROL singers have been banned from wards at Torbay Hospital in case they infect the patients. The 16-strong Gospelaires male voice choir, which has taken Christmas cheer to patients for 40 years, described the ban as 'political correctness gone mad'.

A letter from hospital chief executive Tony Parr said visiting times and regulations had been changed because of 'clear evidence that the risk of infection is usually at its greatest over the winter period'. He added that the hospital can no longer accept offers of Christmas visits by groups.

The move stunned singers and patients alike. Conductor

Colin Reynolds said: 'All the choirmen are very disappoint-ed as this was always one of the highlights of our year. The patients really love to hear us sing and the nurses, too.

'Surely 16 men would not present a health hazard and we would have taken all the hygiene precautions necessary.'

However, Caroline Hill of South Devon Healthcare Trust said the move was popular. 'We have had overwhelm-ing support from public and patients for restricting visiting times and numbers on the wards to lessen the risk of illnesses being brought in,' she said.

barnstapletowncentre.co.uk 8/12/06

No blind eye to baskets

A DISABLED tenant faces having her hanging baskets and flower pots forcibly removed by her housing association on health and safety grounds.

Housing chiefs told a stunned Sharon Kerrigan that the six baskets on her ground-floor flat posed a 'potential risk', as did her plant pots in the communal area at Fredericks Court, King's Road, Beaconsfield.

Asthma sufferer Sharon, 43, who was reduced to tears by the bureaucrats, described the plants as her 'little enjoyment', adding: 'I think it's stupid. They're not a risk — they have been there since I moved in 2000.'

Mrs Kerrigan said she had been told by Paradigm Housing that residents could trip over the pots and tubs in the communal area, for example, during a fire evacuation.

A tearful Mrs Kerrigan said: 'I have chronic asthma so I can't work so it is my little enjoyment. Now that has been taken away from me.'

But Geoff Gigg, Paradigm regional manager, said the unauthorised plants presented his organisation with a number of health and safety issues.

'We have advised her that a further inspection will be carried out shortly with our health and safety manager and if it is felt that there is a potential risk she may well be asked to remove some of her personal items.' This included hanging baskets, he said.

Councillor Geoff Grover defended the move. 'If a postman hit a hanging basket and fell over and hit his head and had a brain haemorrhage and died then Paradigm would be responsible [so] you can understand them then saying we knew about this lady's baskets but turned a blind eye.'

Buck Free Press 20/2/08

Police bill dashes St George

WIGAN'S St George's Day parade has been axed for the first time in its 60-year history after safety fears and a long-running dispute over the cost of policing the event.

Changes to the way marches and parades are organised and policed mean organisers have reluctantly had to cancel the event after discovering it would cost them £1,300.

The decision has been criticised by one of the borough's

top clergymen as yet another erosion of British tradition by bureaucracy. Earlier, Greater Manchester Police said they would stop policing parades in order to concentrate on fighting crime.

District commissioner for the Scout movement in Wigan, Allan Foster, said they could have met the £1,300 costs with fund-raising events – but felt it would be dangerous to have 700 children walking without a police presence.

'We have taken the decision, after risk assessment, that we simply couldn't go ahead. We are saddened that for the first time in more than 60 years this won't happen but we had to think of the safety of the children.'

Leader of the Conservative party in Wigan, Mike Winstanley, branded the situation 'disgraceful' and accused the police of 'distancing themselves from the events and putting the onus on the local authority'.

He added: 'The police are funded by the public to do the job the public want and until they start to do that they'll lose respect. All they seem to be doing is rubbing people up the wrong way.'

Manchester Evening News 29/3/08

Too tight for Xmas cheer

A CHRISTMAS charity band has been ordered to stop playing at a Tesco store for health and safety reasons.

The Guardian Concert Band had been booked to

perform but was halted by security guards after only four carols – accompanied by singing shoppers – and told to leave the store in Blackpool, Lancs.

A spokesperson for the supermarket giant blamed a new policy and 'in-store congestion'.

But band secretary Neil Coleridge-Smith fumed: 'The feeling was that they merely wanted more space for the poinsettia display.'

The Sun 11/12/07

Extinguishers branded safety hazard

FIRE extinguishers could be removed from communal areas in flats throughout the country because they are a safety hazard. Risk assessors in Bournemouth decided the life-saving devices encourage untrained people to fight a fire rather than leave the building.

There are fears that their recommendation, which has seen the extinguishers ripped out of several private high-rise flats in the town, could set a national precedent.

Mike Edwards, who lives in one of the blocks, said he was 'absolutely staggered' that risk experts thought it a safe decision.

'They're worried we will point them in the wrong direction or use the wrong extinguishers.' The 61-year-old claimed his neighbours were now worried sick that a fire could break out.

Dorset Fire and Rescue defended the move, saying:

'Obviously, in some cases, an extinguisher could come in useful but, with new building regulations, every escape route should be completely fireproof.'

Metro.co.uk 10/3/08

Grail chapel bans snaps

PHOTOGRAPHERS have criticised a medieval chapel featured in *The Da Vinci Code* after it banned photography on health and safety grounds, blaming cracked and uneven flooring.

The 15th century chapel near Edinburgh, which is featured in both Dan Brown's book and subsequent film, has long been the subject of legends connected with the Holy Grail. After the film's release in 2006, visitor numbers increased five-fold.

According to Colin Glynne-Percy, director of the Rosslyn Chapel Trust: 'When you have a large group of people wandering around looking at the little screens on digital cameras – and not where they are going – it can lead to people tripping and stumbling.'

But Edinburgh-based photographer Malcolm Fife said it was 'yet another restriction on photographers' and suggested 'it may be a plot to make visitors buy postcards from the large gift shop'.

Photographer Brian Saberton said: 'This seems to be yet another example, not only of the prevailing nanny state mentality, but also of the desire of officialdom to pick on photography as something that needs to be banned.'

A message posted on the chapel's website tells potential visitors: 'Welcome to Rosslyn Chapel. Please note that for the safety, comfort and overall enjoyment of our visitors there is no interior photography or video allowed at Rosslyn Chapel.'

Amateur Photographer 9/1/08

Ladder fear pulls down posters

THE traditional sight of election posters on lamp posts is set to become a thing of the past in Midlothian – for health and safety reasons. Now the council has agreed to impose a ban on the posters at future elections because of the risks involved in putting them up.

The local authority's director of commercial services, John Blair, said the practise of political activists scaling pre-cariously-placed ladders presented 'a clear risk to road users and untrained people erecting and removing posters adjacent to a trafficked road'.

Midlothian Council sent a consultation paper to the Scottish government and Scotland's 32 local authorities seeking guidance on the matter. The Scottish government agreed the posters were unsightly and posed a danger to road users.

However, of the 13 local authorities that responded to the consultation, only Fife and Moray have already taken the same action.

Some of the smaller political parties have been taken aback by the proposals, fearing that they will be further marginalised by the move.

Midlothian Green Party convener Ian Baxter said: 'An amendment to remove or reduce the presence of posters is likely to result in a reduction in turnout as a result of reduced voter awareness of the poll taking place.'

The Scottish Socialist Party branded the action 'fundamentally undemocratic'.

However, Midlothian Provost Adam Montgomery said: 'The sight of young men and women climbing ladders at all times of day and in all weathers is clearly a cause for concern.'

Edinburgh Evening News 23/4/08

Taken for a joy ride

IT HAS taken almost a year and £110,000 of taxpayers' money to produce – but some might feel a day trip to Alton Towers could have come to the same conclusions.

A report for the Health and Safety Executive has found that passengers on amusement rides often stick their hands above their heads to enhance the thrill. Another of the study's main findings is that children like to wave to their parents as they whiz round on carousels.

The report also warns that passengers risk being injured if they stick their arms or legs out of carriages or attempt to stand up.

For the study – 'Passenger Behaviour on Amusement Rides' – the team filmed a range of rides. The 140-page report says: 'The most commonly observed behaviour was one and two handed waving, turning of the head/trunk and pointing. The most common motives were communication, exhibitionism, curiosity and thrill enhancement.'

Behaviour was different depending on age and gender – young adults tended to show 'increased levels of exhibitionism and thrill enhancement' – and females were more likely to wave than males.

Researchers also spotted some 'relatively infrequent' risky behaviour which included sticking their legs out on pirate ship rides and climbing between horses on carousels.

The HSE said: 'There was a gap in knowledge about passenger behaviour and the information can be used by ride designers and operators to reduce accidents.'

This is London 8/8/07

Fire crews scorn bunting

FIREFIGHTERS in Ampthill, Bedfordshire, have been told they cannot use their ladders to take down festive bunting because it is too dangerous.

The town held its annual Gala Day in July and to mark the occasion the historic market town was festooned with colourful bunting.

In previous years, fire brigade officers have pitched in after the event to help remove the decorations but now, nearly four months later and the bunting is still in place.

Councillor Mark Smith said: 'The reason the festival bunting is still up arises from the fact that due to local health and safety advice the local fire brigade is unable to take the bunting down.'

Disgruntled resident Charlie Garth said: 'What the blazes. I'm sure our brave firemen aren't frightened about falling off a piddling little ladder.'

Deputy chief fire officer Graeme Smith put things in perspective: 'Yes, it sounds like the world has gone mad. Firefighters will climb ladders to rescue people from burning buildings but not to remove bunting after a festival.'

Bedfordshire on Sunday 21/10/07

Too early for own funeral

MOURNERS turned up at a funeral to find the coffin had been buried an hour earlier – because of health and safety fears.

The interment at the Hills of Dunipace Cemetery was carried out without family and friends present on the orders of Falkirk Council. The dead man, who was in his mid-30s, was thought to be 6ft 6in and to weigh about 25 stone.

The arrangement left the man's friends shocked and angry. A friend, who asked not to be named, said: 'I was asked by the family to make the arrangements and only heard about the change the day before the funeral.

'I was told it was to do with the weight of the coffin and the council was not prepared to put the men expected to carry the coffin from the hearse to the grave at risk.'

He added: 'We sang hymns and said prayers and it was all really nice, but following a hearse without a coffin to the cemetery later was very unreal.'

The funeral director, Graham Easton, said: 'In nearly 30 years as a funeral director, this is the first time I have been given such a request. I was not happy about it and did not see any need for it.

'Frankly, I found the entire episode quite bizarre,' he said. 'The coffin was large, but by no means unmanageable.'

A spokesperson for Falkirk Council defended the decision. 'In special circumstances, interments take place before the family arrive, to ensure burials are carried out in a safe and dignified manner. In this case, our decision was based on health and safety considerations and to spare the family further distress.'

The Scotsman 27/7/07

Pier drop grounds birdmen

FOR 30 years they have tried to defy gravity by launching themselves off a pier in crazy contraptions. But the Birdmen of Bognor have now come up against a much stronger force – the health and safety brigade.

The plug has been pulled on the International Bognor Birdman Challenge because of council fears that competitors could be injured after pier renovation work left 2ft less water to cover their fall than in previous years.

More than 15,000 spectators normally flock to the East Sussex town to watch madcap aviators in bizarre costumes attempt to fly. But 50ft has been shorn from the pier, meaning competitors have 12ft of water below them instead of 14ft – leaving the council fearing possible compensation claims.

Competition chairman Barry Jones, who had already accepted entrants from Germany and America, said: 'It's the most terrible thing. It's not quite the end of the world but we are pretty depressed. We are apprehensive as to whether it will ever happen in Bognor again.'

Ron 'Bald Eagle' Freeman, 52, from Newcastle, who has won the contest eight times, feels he won't be able to defend his title. 'I am gutted for everyone. It's a terrible day for the Birdman and I hope an alternative venue can be found.'

Bognor Council said it hoped to restore the pier to its previous length to allow the festival to go ahead in future.

Daily Mail 11/4/08

Sound blow to orchestras

MUSICIANS playing in orchestras face being ordered to perform more quietly under new European noise regulations. Some could even be told to wear earplugs, while orchestras will have to play additional quieter pieces during performances under the new European Union health and safety rules.

The Control of Noise at Work Regulations came into force in April 2006 and cap daily or weekly average exposure to 85 decibels. But the music and entertainment industry was given two more years to implement the new rules.

Now a working group, whose members include the English National Opera, the Royal Opera House, Equity, the Health and Safety Executive, and the Musicians' Union, is discussing how the guidelines could apply to the music industry.

The group could suggest that orchestra managers balance loud works by the likes of Wagner and Strauss with quieter pieces by Mozart and Handel and could also encourage musicians to lower the volume during rehearsals.

This would allow them to perform at full volume later without breaking the permitted levels. Individual players could be surrounded by an acoustic screen and musicians could wear earplugs especially designed for orchestras.

Thorben Dittes, projects manager at the Association of British Orchestras, said: 'The most important issue is that we get to protect our players' hearing. There may be scheduling difficulties at the beginning but people will just get used to it.'

Yorkshire Post 1/6/07

End of play

PARENTS in Peterborough are angry about a decision to

close a popular play area in the city after having asked for some improvements. Now Peterborough City Council says it will cost too much to bring it up to European safety rules standards.

Mothers in Norburn say they have made the area the heart of the community.

'If this goes it will be a real loss as the kids will have nowhere to play,' said Sara Hamlet. 'They've made friends out here and it means the nearest place they can play is Bretton Park. It's over a dozen roads to get there and nowhere near where we can keep an eye on them.'

The council said it was reviewing more than 300 play areas to see where the available money should be spent. Spokesperson Elaine Jewell said the work was simply too expensive.

'To make this play area safe would cost about £25,000. Our annual budget for improvements is about £50,000 and we can't really justify spending that much on one play area.'

BBC News 22/10/03

Flip flop flap

TOWN Hall workers hoping to stay chilled in the hot weather have been banned from wearing flip-flops. Staff at Oldham Council are barred from stepping out in the open-style sandals on health and safety grounds.

Bosses claim it will reduce accidents in the workplace – especially trips and falls – but the move has been condemned by employees.

One council worker who has been denied the chance to get some air to his feet said: 'This is health and safety gone mad, but it's no surprise in the current culture of risk assessments.'

Brian Armstrong of trade union Unison said: 'There are jobs where flip-flops are not suitable. But if you are sitting with your feet under a desk, I don't see many problems.'

A spokesperson for the Royal Society for the Prevention of Accidents, added: 'The council should first have evidence that they do cause more accidents.'

Head of civil contingencies, strategic health and safety at the council, Steve Howard, said: 'Oldham Council takes the health and safety of all if its employees very seriously. Council research shows that nearly 50 percent of accidents within the council between April 2006 and March 2007 were the result of slips, trips and falls and moving around.

'By ensuring staff wear suitable footwear for work we hope substantially to reduce this number.'

Manchester Evening News 8/6/07

Library ejects young mum

A YOUNG mum was 'made to feel like a criminal' after being told to leave a college study group – because she had her sleeping baby with her. Staff feared the child might be injured by dust, temperature or hard surfaces.

Liz Cooper, 25, took five-month-old Dominica Jimenez

to a group study session at St Mary's College, Blackburn, but was soon asked to leave by security staff.

Ms Cooper, who is studying in the evening for a degree in early years health, said the college had supported her when pregnant and said she could take the baby in with her for short periods.

She has been told that she may only have Dominica with her in the breast-feeding room or the baby-changing facilities.

'The breast-feeding facilities are all well and good,' said Ms Cooper. 'But if I can't take her onto the rest of the site, what's the point? I'm not going to take her to college just to feed her.'

She described her shock as staff, citing safety concerns, called her away from the group and asked her to leave. 'I was very embarrassed and upset. It was absolute madness and I was made to feel like a criminal.'

Sarah Flanagan, director of development at the college, said Ms Cooper had been given permission to take Dominica into college for short visits, but guidance from the Health and Safety Executive meant they could not allow the baby in the library or other areas.

'Liz was given the opportunity to finish her task at the computer and then left. We are confident that our reception and higher education staff have behaved with the utmost professionalism and are disappointed that Elizabeth feels otherwise.'

Lancashire Telegraph 6/12/07

177

Pupils cross over safety sacking

AN ISLE of Man lollipop man has been suspended for helping school children across two roads instead of one.

Michael Hunt was employed at Marown School to patrol the A1 Peel to Douglas road – but also took children across the nearby busy Glen Darragh Road.

The Department of Transport told him to stop on insurance and safety grounds and suspended him when he refused.

Mr Hunt insists the Glen Darragh Road, just a few yards away from his regular crossing point, is an accident waiting to happen.

'I have been instructed to immediately stop escorting these children across the road,' he said. 'And I have been suspended because I refused to do so.'

In its letter to Mr Hunt, the department said: 'You refused to limit your school crossing patrol activities to the prescribed area.'

The department said it could not comment on personnel issues but added that it was 'continuing to investigate ways of improving road safety on Glen Darragh Road'.

Parents, teachers and pupils are dismayed. 'Mr Hunt is the best lollipop man ever,' said one parent. 'He made the children smile every morning and it's absolutely ridiculous what has happened to him.'

BBC News 11/5/06

Tesco bursts Barney's bubble

A CHILDREN'S entertainer has had his bubble burst after a Leeds supermarket banned him from blowing up balloons in his act.

When Barney Baloney the Clown, real name Tony Turner, was booked to appear at Tesco at Cross Gates he was told to leave his balloons at home.

For seven years, the 47-year-old professional children's entertainer has twisted a bagful of balloons into animal shapes to hand to children as part of his act.

Mr Turner from Sheffield was told that balloons had been banned by Tesco because the latex they contain could harm children.

It is more bad news for Mr Turner whose act has already suffered after he was forced to stop using a bubble-making machine.

He was refused public liability cover because insurance companies said the bubbles might cause the children to slip and hurt themselves.

Mr Turner said: 'At this rate I will have no act left. Things are going from crazy to ridiculous. Twisting balloons into shapes makes up 40 percent of my act and I can't see what the problem is. Kids love to see me make shapes and that part of my act is the children's favourite.'

The father-of-three added: 'This country is going crazy with its political correctness and health and safety issues and it's making us a laughing stock.'

A Tesco spokesperson confirmed that this was a health and safety issue. 'We have banned balloons because latex is used in the manufacture of them and this can trigger an allergic reaction in some children. We always have the welfare of children at heart.'

Yorkshire Evening Post 14/7/07

Earmuffs for binmen

THE Health and Safety Executive is urging councils to issue binmen with earmuffs to protect their hearing while collecting bottles and jars for recycling. It also recommends that they empty the boxes slowly to lessen the noise.

The legal noise threshold is 87 decibels a day, but the HSE found that binmen emptying 50 boxes of glass a day into a metal dustcart are exposed to 89dB and it says the 'high levels of noise' could lead to 'permanent hearing damage'.

It says employers must 'provide hearing protectors that are simple to remove and replace as required, for example canal caps or earmuffs'.

Daily Telegraph 22/1/09

Binmen fear heights

A FRAIL pensioner has been told her rubbish won't be collected – because health and safety rules prevent her burly binmen from lifting her bin over a 4in step.

Priscilla Thomas, 76, who is just 5ft and weighs 6 stone, is expected to put the wheelie bin out herself – but fears she is so frail she will lose control of it.

Now her rubbish has been left to pile up outside her home in Elizabeth Avenue, Hove. 'It's bureaucracy gone out of control,' she said.

When she confronted the bin men to ask why her rubbish was not being removed, she was astounded to hear that the tiny step was deemed a health and safety hazard and they were not allowed to pull the bin down it.

'I live on a hill and if I try to roll the bin out into the street for them to collect, it might overbalance and spill rubbish everywhere,' she said. 'Also, leaving it on the pavement creates an obstacle for pedestrians, especially those with pushchairs and wheelchairs and for blind people.'

Mrs Thomas said the situation has left her feeling as if she is banging her head against a brick wall. 'My neighbour has the same type of step and his bin gets collected, so why doesn't mine?'

Brighton Argus 17/12/07

Coastguard hero drops out

A HEROIC coastguard who risked his life to save a 13-year-old girl trapped on a cliff ledge has quit after bosses criticised him for breaching health and safety rules during the daring rescue.

Volunteer coastguard Paul Waugh, 44, climbed down a cliff without safety equipment in gale force winds to rescue Faye Harrison, 13, who had become trapped.

Mr Waugh, from East Cleveland, won a string of awards for his bravery the previous year.

But bosses at the Maritime and Coastguard Agency (MCA) said that Mr Waugh had breached health and safety regulations by not using safety equipment. After 13 years of dedicated work as a volunteer coastguard, Mr Waugh claims he was forced to quit the job after pressure from above.

'The way I have been treated is terrible,' says Mr Waugh. 'I loved that job and I am absolutely gutted that I am leaving. A girl's life was in imminent danger and I did what I had to save her life. But my bosses didn't see it that way – they said I should have waited for support and safety equipment.'

Faye from Saltburn-by-the-sea, East Cleveland, said she was disgusted by the way Paul had been treated. 'If he hadn't been brave enough to climb down to me I don't think I would be here today. Paul is a hero.'

A spokesperson for MCA said: 'We wish Paul well in his future endeavours and the MCA is very grateful for his past activities and work in the Coastguard Rescue Service. However, the MCA is very mindful of health and safety regulations which are in place for very good reasons.'

Northern Echo 11/1/08

Treetop Teddies get the chop

THE PICNIC is over for a treetop teddy bear display at Bollington tip. Waste workers had lovingly assembled the tableau – made up of abandoned cuddly toys – to add a touch of colour to the site.

But their quirky scene, admired by the town's children, has now been foiled by a county council banning order.

In a move branded 'ridiculous' by tip workers, their stuffed animal assortment, salvaged from the rubbish at Bollington Household Waste and Recycling Centre, had to be torn down from the branches after the council called it an 'eyesore'.

One worker, who asked to remain anonymous, said: 'The council said it was an eyesore and a potential distraction to people driving into the tip, which made it a health and safety issue. But we thought it was a nice feature and the children loved it. It made people feel relaxed. They're just being killjoys.'

A County Hall spokesperson said: 'Our waste and recycling sites need to be kept clean and tidy and the display didn't fit in with a professional image.'

The creative crew have made previous attempts to display dumped goods but have been foiled on each occasion by the council.

A centre manager added: 'We were only trying to make the centre more cheerful. People seemed more willing to recycle and they went home happy. We should be praised, not told off.'

Macclesfield Express 30/4/08

Hero fights to keep compensation

JUDGES have attacked a fire authority which asked for an injured fireman to be denied compensation because he 'should not have attempted to save a driver's life'.

John Pennington was involved in a desperate bid to free a trapped driver following a multiple pile-up on the M25. During the rescue attempt the experienced firefighter lost part of his left forefinger while using a power ram in a last-ditch effort to save the stricken motorist, who later died.

He was awarded compensation, but Surrey fire officials said Mr Pennington should never have been involved in the rescue attempt as he was not trained to use the equipment.

Appealing against the pay-out, Surrey Fire Service and Surrey County Council have spent thousands of pounds arguing firemen must put their own safety first, even if that means abandoning accident victims to their fate.

But judges at the Court of Appeal dismissed the claim as 'unrealistic', saying Mr Pennington had 'acted reasonably' in attempting to save the driver's life.

A judge awarded Mr Pennington, of Selsey, West Sussex, £3,115 compensation for the injury. But county fire officials have since spent several times the sum on an unsuccessful legal bid to strip the firefighter of his pay-out.

Fire officials claimed it was Mr Pennington's decision to use the ram and that firefighters 'must put their own health and safety first, however unpalatable the consequences'.

The court found otherwise, with one of the judges adding: 'Not only is it unrealistic to conclude that Mr Pennington should not have continued with the rescue attempt, but he did what was expected of him.'

Daily Mail 10/10/06

Chainsaw tree massacre

OVER-ZEALOUS council chiefs are ripping out the ancient trees that line Britain's streets and parks because of misguided fears about health and safety. A damning government report warns that trees are being chopped down in urban areas more quickly than they are being planted.

The 'chainsaw massacre' is being fuelled by the UK's compensation culture and fears that falling branches could lead to expensive insurance claims.

Eric Pickles, the Shadow Secretary of State for Communities and Local Government, warned that the leafy character of urban areas was under threat.

'Whitehall's failure to tackle the compensation culture and the heavy-handed application of health and safety regulation is doing more harm than good,' he said.

'Trees have a vital role to play in tackling climate change and improving quality of life, yet Britain's leafy suburbs face a chainsaw massacre under Labour.'

Councils around Britain have uprooted trees on the grounds that their leaves pose a 'trip hazard' and that insect droppings can lead to infectious diseases. In Bristol, the local authorities chopped down 100 newly-planted yew trees amid fears that eating their leaves in quantity might lead to illness.

The new report – published by the Department of

Communities and Local Government – is the biggest ever survey of urban trees in England.

The report warned: 'Although concerns about public safety will always restrict the number of mature and over-mature trees along roads and highways, policies for routine removal of all large trees during the early phases of maturity and their replacement with smaller 'safer' alternatives should be challenged.

'The importance of mature and ancient trees in urban areas is undeniable and local authorities responsible for their management must balance public safety against their responsibilities for protecting and enhancing the environment.'

Daily Mail 19/2/08

Ducks fall foul of red tape

PLASTIC ducks have been launched from a dam in Lymm, near Warrington, every Easter Monday for 15 years to raise money for charity. But now the river will be empty after the event fell foul of red tape.

More than 1,000 people watched the previous race which raised thousands of pounds for good causes. But organisers at Lymm and District Round Table were told they will now have to pay about £3,000 for road closures within the village to ensure the event runs smoothly.

Resident Peter Davies said: 'The duck race has become an Easter tradition and everyone is really upset it's not happening. It raises lots of money for local charities and last year's was the biggest ever.'

The decision was made by the safety committee at Warrington council, whose consent was needed for insurance to be valid. Round Table members would have struggled to raise the necessary sum – almost as much as the total raised by last year's event.

Chairman James Phipps said: 'We're disappointed that this has had to happen after 15 incident-free years. I don't hold the council responsible – it comes down to a wider paranoia about litigation. But the cost of these closures made the duck race quite prohibitive. If we had a poor turnout due to the weather we would end up out of pocket.'

A council spokesperson said: 'Unfortunately, we have many competing priorities and our budget simply could not stretch to cover the duck race as well.'

Manchester Evening News 6/4/07

Gag on market traders

STALL-holders in the market town of Hexham in Northumberland have been told to keep their noise down because the volume is causing a health and safety hazard for nearby office-workers.

Tynedale District Council acted quickly after receiving 'several complaints' and sent letters to each of the stall-holders asking them to reduce the volume and frequency of their calls.

'There have been instances when the noise of the market became more than office workers could cope with,' explained a spokesperson for the council. 'We haven't banned the market sellers from shouting at any time, we have just asked them to quieten down.'

The traders, who pay nearly £1,000 rent for a stall, said attempts to change the character of the market threaten its very survival.

'It's ridiculous. Hexham's supposed to be a market town,' explained fruit and veg trader Martin Foster, 29. 'If we can't attract customers, particularly in winter, then I'm worried the stall might not survive.'

Hexham market, which sells fruit and veg, bric-a-brac, clothing and pet supplies, attracts visitors from all over the country.

'They put on a fabulous display, even though not enough people come here any more,' said fishmonger Carolyn Ridley. 'The traders' cries are part of the colour of the market.'

Hexham market was established in 1239 with the approval of Henry III.

Sky News 18/8/08

Safety hinders mail

BRITAIN'S 'universal' post service – the obligation to provide a 'one-price-goes-anywhere' distribution of letters and parcels across the country – is under threat because of increased health and safety fears.

According to industry watchdog Postwatch, the number of households receiving no post because of problems such as slippery paths, overgrown hedges or letterboxes that slam shut too hard has gone up 12-fold in four years.

In 2004, just 22 addresses across the entire country were blacklisted on 'short-term' health and safety grounds. By 2006, that figure had risen to 167. In 2007, there were 262 'exceptions'.

'Of course health and safety is very important but the risks associated with delivering letters shouldn't be exaggerated,' insists Andy Frewin of Postwatch. 'If it's safe for a family to live in a house, is it really reasonable to suggest it is too dangerous for letters to be delivered?'

Daily Mail 23/8/08

Danger: dodgy bridge

JUST when you thought there was no area of British life left for the health and safety lobby to invade, they've found another one – the game of bridge. A 46-page *Be Safe* guide has been declared essential reading for people learning the sedate card game.

The booklet, published by government quango the Learning and Skills Council at a cost of £165,000, is issued to adult education establishments and aims to 'raise awareness amongst learners about risk' and tells them to 'always close drawers' and 'clean up spills straight away'.

Astonishingly, it also urges readers to dry their hands on a towel rather than their clothes and to take chewing gum out of their mouths before eating. One page simply repeats the words *Be Safe* over and over again.

Retired company director Roger Handley, 60, was among baffled would-be bridge players at an adult education institute in East Finchley, North London, who were given the glossy booklet during their first lesson.

He said: 'The poor guy teaching us said he was legally obliged to give us the guide. We had to sign to say we'd received it. It is a waste of time and money. The government doesn't trust us to think.'

Be Safe, which costs 22p a copy to produce, contains a quiz that poses questions such as: 'If the fire alarm rings just as you are about to start your lunch hour should you wait until you finish your sandwiches before leaving the building?'

Anyone who successfully completes the quiz qualifies for a certificate.

Mail on Sunday 28/10/06

Hands-free policing

POLICE officers have been warned not to hold out a hand to drowning swimmers and to think twice before throwing a lifebelt in case they are pulled into the water themselves.

The health and safety rules issued by Devon and Cornwall Constabulary state an officer on the bank of a

river or lake must not help struggling non-swimmers.

Even a life belt must not be thrown without a 'dynamic risk assessment' being carried out. Where possible, rescues should be left to other emergency services.

In another case, two Dorset police officers carrying life-saving equipment were ordered not to board a lifeboat to reach a suspected heart attack victim because they were not trained in sea survival.

Daily Telegraph 19/4/08

Raisin floors safety official

THEY spend their time trying to protect us from unnecessary dangers – but it seems health and safety officials are as accident prone as the rest of us. Injury statistics reveal that workers at the Health and Safety Executive have been involved in a series of bizarre mishaps.

One employee slipped on a raisin while another cut his head when he walked into a warning sign. In a separate accident, a worker bruised her eye when a lavatory-paper dispenser fell from the wall.

The figures, released under the Freedom of Information Act, show there were more than 500 accidents and injuries involving the organisation's 3,500 employees over three years, a rate of about one every two days.

There were 154 slips, trips or falls. A wet tea-room floor caused a groin strain, while another worker pulled a hamstring. Another twisted her ankle after falling off a kerb, while other employees suffered minor burns from a toaster and after accidentally touching a light bulb.

A spokesperson for the Health and Safety Executive defended its safety record.

'It would be unreasonable to expect that an organisation that employs more than 3,500 people would suffer no injuries,' he said.

Daily Mail 8/3/07